DEFYING
GRAVITY

Prill Boyle

DEFYING GRAVITY

A CELEBRATION
of LATE-BLOOMING WOMEN

PRILL BOYLE

To my mother...a patient and loving gardener, who taught me to delight not only in the snowdrop, which blooms at the first hint of spring and then quickly disappears, but also in the graceful Japanese anemone, which begins to show its colors in late summer—long after most other perennials have faded—and then blossoms until the first frosts of fall. My mother would call the women in this book "late bloomers."

CONTENTS

THE WOMEN

LINDA BACH / 19

At fifty, Linda Bach fulfilled a lifelong dream and became a medical doctor.

IRMA ELDER / 35

At fifty-two, housewife Irma Elder became the first woman to run an automobile franchise in Detroit.

JEAN KELLEY / 53

At forty-nine, after spending two years on welfare and leaving an abusive marriage, Jean Kelley earned a Ph.D. and became an interim dean of students at a community college.

JO FUCHS LUSCOMBE / 77

At forty-eight, homemaker and community volunteer Jo Fuchs Luscombe was elected to the first of five terms as a Connecticut State Representative.

i

"FUNDAMENTALLY SPEAKING, GRAVITY IS AN
EXTREMELY FEEBLE FORCE."
—Brian Greene, *The Elegant Universe*

INTRODUCTION

Whether we're in the first flowering of adulthood or the autumn of our lives, most of us long to do something that energizes us and fills us with joy. We hope to make a difference, to leave a seed of ourselves behind to germinate in future generations. But all too often, we settle for far less and toil away at jobs that are smaller than our spirits. We tell ourselves that we aren't young enough, educated enough, talented enough or rich enough to do what we really want. Convinced that it's impractical, even childish, to listen to our hearts, we travel so far from our desire that when it speaks to us, we no longer recognize the sound. Worse yet, we stop dreaming altogether. But following the call of our heart is not a luxury reserved for a select few. It is our birthright.

Before I began writing this book, I thought I had already blossomed. Tired of being a secretary, I went to Georgetown University to earn a degree in English. I didn't graduate until I was thirty-eight. By the time I was in my mid-forties, I had a devoted husband, wonderful children and a job teaching writing at a community college in Connecticut. But deep inside myself I knew I wasn't using my talents to their fullest. I still had love to spare.

Then one morning I asked my students to draft an essay. "Imagine you're ninety," I said. "What sort of person did you become? How did you use your gifts?" I encouraged them to be playful in their response—not to worry about how much money they had or how many years it would take to master a skill. I hoped that by viewing their lives from a distance, their dreams would come into focus.

To inspire them, I related an interview with a centenarian I'd heard on National Public Radio. Asked if she had any regrets about her life, she paused for a moment and replied, "If I had I known I would live to be a hundred, I would have taken up the violin at forty. By now I could have been playing for sixty years!"

Truthfully, we don't know how much time we have left. Not one breath can be taken for granted. But when we allow ourselves the possibility of living almost a century, all sorts of things we thought we were too old to do suddenly seem worth attempting.

Whether any of my students became braver with their dreams from doing this assignment, I can't honestly say. But I did. I pictured myself on an archeological dig in Turkey and having a vacation home in Maine. I also envisioned becoming a successful author.

As I was writing, I didn't take my words seriously. But when I read my essay to the class, a young man raised his hand and asked whether I'd ever published anything. He kidded that if I hadn't, I'd better get started. I felt as though an angel had tapped me on the shoulder and whispered in my ear, "Time to wake up, Prill." Until that moment, I'd never really acknowledged my desire to be a writer.

Not long after, I spotted an article in *The New York Times* about a sixty-five year old Kentucky woman named Wini Yunker. She had waited thirty-nine years to fulfill her dream of joining the Peace Corps and was leaving the States that day for a two-year assignment in Ukraine. The article provided a lot of biographical details, but neglected to explain the origin of this woman's courage. I wanted to hear her story firsthand.

Unable at that point to get in touch with Wini, I asked myself, "Wouldn't it be wonderful if I could locate other late-blooming women and let them tell their stories in their own words?" I thought their in-depth accounts might inspire my students, who often take years to achieve their goals. I didn't want to write about famous women with lives far removed from everyday people. I wanted to write about ordinary women with the kind of extraordinary persistence and courage it takes to join the Peace Corps at sixty-five.

From that day onward, this book became my passion. I could imagine a picture of a woman on the cover, a dedication to my mother on the first page, and a quote at the beginning of each chapter. My vision was that clear. But translating inspiration into action proved to be no small challenge. Discouraged by my slow progress, I began to think that maybe I'd set my sights too high. The mere thought of putting pen to paper made me tremble. And while I managed to gather the names of a few late bloomers, I was too intimidated to pick up the phone and call them.

A year went by and procrastination turned into panic. Like a parent admonishing a child, I looked at myself in the mirror one day and yelled, "You fool! You're wasting a precious opportunity." In my heart, I knew I would never forgive myself if I didn't at least attempt to write.

I finally picked up the list of names I'd compiled over the previous year and arranged to meet a woman who'd become a doctor at fifty. She graduated from medical school the same year her daughter graduated from college. Compared to her perseverance, my own struggles seemed insignificant. I was so inspired that I couldn't wait to interview the next woman on my list.

More than two years after reading her profile in the *Times*, I was able at last to reach Wini Yunker. In April of 2002 she graciously invited me to Kentucky to hear her story.

Like Wini, all the wonderful women I've interviewed took years to display their full array of colors. Jo Fuchs Luscombe, a former state representative and House whip, had never even taken charge of a PTA committee before moving to Connecticut in her mid-thirties. Patricia Symonds, a professor of anthropology at Brown University, didn't graduate from high school until she was in her forties. Jane Work began her career as a Gestalt therapist in her mid-sixties and just retired last year at eighty-four. Some of these women were poor; others had no money concerns. Linda Bach worried about hot flashes, but not tuition bills. Jean Kelley, always strapped for cash, found several creative ways to finance her endeavors.

Ultimately, the twelve women in this book became my role models. They taught me to focus on my goal rather than obstacles and encouraged me to celebrate being a woman on the cusp of fifty. Immersed in their tales of late blooming, I gradually sprouted my own tender shoots and began to think that maybe I, too, had a story worth telling.

I eventually decided to include excerpts from the journal I started at the beginning of this project. Just as these women had faced their fears, I was now facing mine. And although my hurdles and setbacks were different from theirs, the joy I felt in overcoming them was much the same. I thought it would be interesting for others to hear not only how I met the women and what I learned, but also to witness firsthand the step-by-step process of a dream coming true.

This book, in other words, is about hope. If you think you're too old or too weighed down to fly, the stories that follow may dispel your doubts.

JOURNAL ENTRY 1

I've decided to write about late-blooming women and to keep a journal of the experience. This is my first entry. I don't know a thing about book writing or even how to locate late bloomers, but a ball was pitched to me and I'm taking a swing. Last night I was so excited about the prospect that I couldn't sleep. When I finally dozed off, I had this dream:

I was in my backyard hosting a large party when suddenly I felt weary from all the socializing and thought to myself, "What the heck. Why not fly?" So I spread my arms wide and very softly, very gently pumped them up and down until I began to rise above the crowd. Higher and higher I went until I was eye level with the tallest tree on our property, a one-hundred-year-old copper beech. I could see Long Island Sound in the distance, and I was able to distinguish the people below. But I couldn't hear a word. So quiet. So free.

Slowly I came out of my reverie—brought back to earth by a tinge of guilt over abandoning my guests. The moment my feet touched the ground, people started coming up to me asking how I had learned to fly. I couldn't answer them. I had always known how. I had just never done it with anyone watching.

After mingling for a while, I noticed several people looking up. In the sky were a dozen of my friends and neighbors.

The alarm went off and I woke up. Lying in bed, I wondered: Had they learned by watching me? Or had they, too, always known how to fly?

"A JOURNEY OF A THOUSAND MILES MUST
BEGIN WITH A SINGLE STEP."   —Lao-Tzu

LINDA BACH

PHYSICIAN

Fulfilling a lifelong dream, Linda Bach became a doctor at age fifty. Elected president of her class, she graduated from medical school the same year her daughter graduated from college. She is now in private practice in Miami Shores, Florida.

As she shares her story, her words frequently spill into ripples of laughter. With sparkling brown eyes and soft, frosted curls that brush against her shoulders, she doesn't look like a typical doctor. She looks like a woman who would hold you if you started to cry.

Before I became a doctor, I was happy with my life. I had a really good marriage. I had a beautiful child. I had a nice house. Everything was fine. But I felt like there was a lot of love put into me that was somehow being wasted.

I grew up as an only child in Springfield, Ohio—a little town of about eighty-thousand people. My mom was thirty-eight and my dad was forty-eight when I was born. When I was seven, my dad had his first heart attack. After that, there was a feeling of illness in the house and a fear that he was going to die. That tension was always there. When I was in fifth grade, he had his third heart attack and was rushed to the hospital. He died a week later.

For years I remembered the date: April 10, 1958. But then I sort of tried to block it out because whenever I'd think about my dad, I'd start crying. I went through a period where I wondered how there could be a God. If there was a God, why would God take my father away? It didn't make sense to me.

The year after my dad died, we took some intelligence tests at my school. I must have done okay because the principal took me aside one day and said, "You know, Linda, you can do whatever you want to do in life." I remember taking that thought home with me and thinking, "Wow, you know, I'd really like to be a heart doctor. Wouldn't it be nice to keep other little girls from losing their dads?" When I first had the nerve to say that aloud, people would tell me, "Oh no, you mean you want to be a nurse." I thought, "No, if I can do anything, I want to be a doctor."

I didn't have a dad who might have encouraged me, and my mom had never gone to college; so all the way through high school, I hung onto the principal's words. I took advanced math and advanced science, and even though people kept telling me I couldn't be a doctor, my desire ran too deep for their comments to deter me.

After I graduated in '65, I enrolled at Ohio State University. A lot of people chose Miami University of Ohio because it was considered the Ivy League of the Midwest. But I'd heard that if I really wanted to be a doctor, I should go to Ohio State, since that's where the medical school was.

Pre-med back then was extremely competitive. There were very few women in the program. Sometimes, in a course like physics, I would be the only female in the class. The grades were curved, but I did just as well as the men. In those days, I had bleached blond hair and always sat in the front. One time after the teacher returned my paper, I heard some guy in the back of the room whisper to his friends, "That dumb blonde in the front got a 100!"

I graduated from Ohio State in 1969 and hoped to go to medical school there the next year. Not everyone got an interview, but my grades were good enough that I guess they felt they had to give me a chance. For the interview, I didn't put on any makeup and pulled my hair back in a bun. Mini-skirts were just coming into fashion, but I wore a suit that was really long, below my knees. I tried to frump up to fit the image these guys wanted.

The interview took place in an old room with dark paneling. There was a long conference table with three men on one side, three on the other and one at the end. I was twenty years old and a nervous wreck. Just to sit there took everything I had. Then these men started asking me whether I planned on getting married and having children— questions that are illegal to ask today. When I said, "Yes, after I finish school and am established in a practice," this man sitting next to me—every square inch of him covered with about a hundred wrinkles—mumbled under his breath, "God, I'd hate to be your kids." He actually said that. I thought to myself, "This is not going well."

One of the men then asked what kind of doctor I wanted to be. People had advised me ahead of time that I should say I wanted to be a pediatrician, because pediatrics was one of the few specialties where it was acceptable to be a woman back then. But I couldn't do that. It wouldn't have been honest. I knew what I wanted to do. I wanted to be a heart doctor. Even more the male domain—heart surgery. Still, I told the truth.

The interview was in December. Then I had to wait for my answer. It was a rolling admissions thing. The longer you waited, the worse your chances. Finally in April I got this thin, little envelope saying they were sorry.

I was just absolutely devastated. My mom had always told me that if you really, really want something and give it your best, you'll get it. God will grant you what you most want. I'd done that, and it didn't work. I remember lying on the couch and crying and crying until I couldn't cry anymore. The shock of it was just so unbelievable. If it hadn't been for my husband Bill, who was my boyfriend then, and my two girlfriends, who were my roommates, I probably would have had a nervous breakdown.

I went back to my college counselor, but she didn't really counsel me. She must have thought it was some whim I had and that I would realize my foolishness and get married. She should have told me to apply to more than one place—schools like the Medical College for Women near Philadelphia. She also should have encouraged me to work on a master's degree. A lot of people would have gone back, done more courses and applied again to show that they were really serious about wanting to go to medical school. When I didn't get in, I just thought that was it.

I graduated with a degree in microbiology and got a job working in a lab at Riverside Hospital in Columbus, Ohio. Looking at bacteria all day was pretty boring. The most exciting part was when I got to take my little basket and go upstairs each morning and draw blood. And, of course, that was what I liked best, to be with the patients. But it was also kind of difficult because I would always see the doctors. I worked in the lab from the time I graduated in '69 until Bill and I got married in February of 1970.

Bill was in the Air Force when we got married, and for a while we were stationed in England. I tutored soldiers and enrolled in some biochemistry classes at Oxford University. As the Vietnam War was scaling down, the Air Force offered Bill an early out. He took it and we moved back to the States, eventually settling in Florida, where Bill got a job as a commercial pilot.

In 1975, our daughter, Sashi, was born. For the next six years or so, I was a full-time wife and mother. I loved it. I'd never been around kids and became like a lioness or something. I never put Sashi down. I would lie in bed and read to her for hours—before she even knew what the words meant!

When Sashi turned six and started school, I told Bill that I was going crazy. He said, "Go take a course." Sashi really liked computers, so I thought it would be neat to take a computer class over at Barry University in Miami Shores. But when Bill and Sashi dropped me off for my first class, I started to cry. I said to Bill, "Look at all these people. They're young. They know what they're doing, and I'm like an imbecile. I can't go in there."

We squished into this bathroom—Bill, Sashi and I—and Bill said to me, "Look, Linda. You can do this. These are just people. Just go in. If you don't like it, leave. It's not as if you're going to see these people again." I didn't want to create a bad example for Sashi, so I finally went to class.

I ended up doing so well that I took more courses. My teachers would say things like, "I can only give you an A because there isn't any grade higher than that." Before I knew it, I had a Master's degree in computer education. Getting started—that's always the hard part. Once you get going, it's just a matter of continuing to make that effort. I was in my mid-thirties when I graduated.

After I got my master's, Sashi's principal hired me to teach computers. Then, when Sashi entered high school, a part-time position for an algebra teacher opened up at her new school. I took the job, but the position ended after a year. It was kind of upsetting. I had to decide if I wanted to go back to school and get certified to teach or do something else.

Right around this time we went on vacation to the Cayman Islands. While we were there, we met some medical students who were taking a break after finishing their boards. We got to talking and somehow I mentioned that I'd always wanted to go to medical school.

One of them spoke up: "Well, why don't you go now?"

I said, "What do you mean now? I can't go now."

"Why not? he said. "They sometimes accept older people to med school. There's this fireman in our class who's thirty-seven."

"Well, I'm a little older than that," I blurted out. I was forty-two or forty-three by then.

That was the end of the conversation. But when we got back home, I kept thinking about what this person had said. I told Bill, "You know, I have to check this out." So I went down to the University of Miami School of Medicine and made an appointment with the director of admissions. I wasn't nervous. I was just going to ask whether it was true that they accepted older people. The director said, "Oh yes. We call them mature students, but you'll have to re-take all your pre-med courses before applying."

That night, sitting in the kitchen, I said to Bill, "Should I go for my teaching certificate, or should I take some courses and do this whole pre-med thing? I mean we're talking a long haul here."

And Bill looked at me and said, "No, we're not talking a long haul. We're only talking one step. Just take one course. If you like it, you like it. If it feels right, it feels right. If it doesn't feel right, then stop."

"That would be okay?" I said. "You wouldn't mind? You're going to pay for this? I mean, I wouldn't be working."

Bill said, "No, it's fine. Just do it. We'll get by."

The first semester I signed up for general chemistry and general biology. Driving up there, I went through that whole thing again of, "Oh my God, Oh my God!" and thinking I was going to look like everyone's mother. But when I walked into that first chemistry class and the teacher started talking about the periodic table, all of a sudden I felt like I had been an amputee—that my arm had been amputated and someone was finally putting it back on. I pulled my hair over my eyes and started to cry.

Again, I did really well in my classes. I couldn't understand why I was doing so well. I guess the truth is that I had a lot of preparation for this. I had a degree in microbiology and I'd done those computer courses. Also, I'd been helping Sashi, who was taking advanced classes at a tough private high school. That sort of kept my brain working. Sashi and I were actually taking physics at the same time. She had the same book I had, only my course lasted ten weeks and hers lasted a year. We'd sit at the kitchen table, and her feet would be on my lap and my feet would be on her chair, and we'd both study physics together.

As I was getting close to finishing my pre-med courses, I decided to check with the admissions people at the University of Miami to make sure I was on the right track. I drove down and showed the dean my transcripts. She took one look at them and said, "Oh, this is good. This is really good. Just keep it up." Then, almost as an afterthought, she added, "You know, you have to do really well on your MCATS (the Medical College Admissions Test). If you do, I might be able to sell you to the admissions committee. We've never accepted anyone as old as you, though, so you only have one shot at this."

I came home and had to lie on the couch. I was so stressed. I ended up with a fever the night before the test. I thought, "This is it." The exam took seven hours and had sections on chemistry, physics and biology. There was also an essay. Then, I had to wait for the grades. When my scores finally came, I was too nervous to open the envelope. I sat on the bed and made Bill read the results. They were really good.

When I took my scores back to the dean, she said, "This is great. Now I can get you an interview." She then grabbed my hand —she was quite a large woman—and marched me down the hallway to the director of admissions' office. "I want Linda to have an interview," she told him. "It may not go anywhere from there, but at least give her an interview."

My interview was really incredible because it was with this kind, grandfatherly black man who was in charge of minority affairs at the university. He was sensitive to discrimination. I told him that I'd always dreamed of becoming a doctor and just wanted to be given a chance. In my application essay I'd said that my book of life was only half-written. I still had many empty pages left. Most people applying had hardly any of their pages filled; theirs were almost completely empty. But my book was still half empty. I told this man that I just wanted to bring in all my experience and practice medicine at the other end of my life.

The interview went well. After we finished, I told him, "You know what? Even if I don't get in, at least you've erased that horrible memory of my other interview. At least I feel I've been given a fair shot."

All those years I felt like I'd disappointed God. Something in me felt I was supposed to be a doctor, but that somehow—the circumstances, Ohio State, whatever—I'd made the wrong choice and was going to have to be lying on my deathbed and saying to God, "You know, I'm sorry." But now I was getting above A's in everything. This was my maximum effort. If I didn't get in this time, it just wasn't meant to be.

The interview took place in late fall. Again, it was a rolling admissions thing and there was a waiting period. The call came right before Christmas, and I remember picking up the phone. The director of admissions was on the line. He said, "How would you like to join the Class of 1997?"

In September of 1993, I entered medical school. Sashi started college the same year. The first day I put on a plaid suit, walked into the auditorium and sat down in the last row. I thought someone would come up to me and say, "What are you doing here? You know mothers really aren't supposed to come with their kids to class." But, of course, I had to see and hear well, so I moved to the front.

A month later I turned forty-six. We had a genetics professor who always asked if it was anyone's birthday. There happened to be two other people who had birthdays on the same day as mine, so all three of us raised our hands. The professor went to the first and said, "How old are you?"

The girl, who was in something called the "Baby Doc" program, replied, "Twenty."

The other person, a young man, said, "I'm twenty-three."

Then the professor came to me. I thought, "Oh God, should I lie, should I refuse to tell my age, or should I just tell the truth?" I said, "Well, I'm forty-six." The whole class burst out in applause.

Not too long after this, a few of the students approached me and said, "We think you should run for president of the class. You've been a teacher, and you'd be really good at negotiating with our professors. We all come to you for advice anyway." I ran and won. It was really cool. It added a whole other dimension to the thing.

On top of everything else, in my second year I started going through menopause. My periods were getting irregular and I was really hungry. Everyone was asking for sweaters, and I'd say, "What are you talking about? It's really warm in here." They're all bundled up and I'm taking my sweater off! It was hilarious. But then I read that some women have memory problems in menopause. I thought, "Oh no, not now!" So I went on hormones.

After two years of classes, I started clinical rotations at Jackson Memorial Hospital. I thought it would be hard staying up all night. But it was actually easier, I think, for me than for some of the younger students. You know when you're a mother and your kid is sick and you're up all night with them? It was like that. I used to stay up all night with Sashi when she was sick. It was no big deal.

Being a mother is like a fast education in selflessness. As a mother, I brought things to the table that couldn't be put on paper and graded. Never, ever did I boss a nurse. I'd say, "Do you have time to help me?" And because I'd had the experience of losing a father and, by then, also a mother, I wanted to be there when a patient was dying.

I remember one lady whose husband was hurting too much to stay with her. We had taken her off the ventilator and started a morphine drip. I didn't want her to die alone, so I held her hand and just talked to her. I also opened up the drapes and let in the sunshine. It seemed to me what any normal person would have done. But later the nurses said, "We've never seen a doctor do that."

Another time, someone's mother was dying. The family was standing around crying, and I was crying with them. People told me, "You're not supposed to cry when you're a doctor." And I said, "Why not? This is a very human moment. I can still be strong and put her on the medicine she needs." The son was trying to put his arms around his mom to hug her, but she had all these tubes in her. He thought she was going to break. I explained to him, "Look, everything is sewed in. Nothing is going to fall out." I showed him how he could get one arm around here and the other arm around there. He was giving her his last hug.

The sickest of the sick are at Jackson Memorial. Other doctors seemed to anesthetize themselves to the pain they saw around them, but my personality was already formed. Even though my heart was ripping apart to see all the suffering, I used to tell the nurses, "If you see me being callous, kick me. Remind me. I don't want to be hard. I want to feel it."

Throughout all these years, Bill never, ever complained. Before going to medical school, I used to pay the bills, run the errands, and take the dog to the vet. Bill was flying and he was gone a lot. But all of a sudden he was home more, and he said, "I'll take over." He didn't really know how to cook at first, but he learned. He drew the line at cleaning the house, though. He said, "Forget it. I'm not doing toilets. We're hiring someone to clean!"

We were remodeling in the middle of this, and he made me a study with pocket doors. For four years, all Bill saw of me was the back of my head as I sat at my desk and studied. Even when we went to the theater, I'd have my anatomy cards tucked inside my purse. We'd be waiting for the show to begin, and I'd be sitting there doing flash cards.

I remember one Fourth of July we were planning to watch the fireworks from our boat. The food was on board. Bill and Sashi were on board. But my surgery exam was the next day, and I said to them, "You know what? I can't go. It could make the difference between passing and failing." I know that sounds bizarre. What difference would two or three hours make? But it did make a difference because there was so much to learn and I needed every second.

I was fifty when I finished. To be a heart doctor, I would have had to do an additional four or five years of cardiology on top of the three years of residency in internal medicine. I didn't want to wait that long to practice. As it turns out, I like the idea of being more of a generalist, taking care of the whole body and not just a little part of it.

At my graduation, because I was the president of the class, I got to give a little speech. Introducing me, the head of the school told the audience that I was unique because not only was I the oldest resident physician at Jackson Memorial Hospital but my daughter was graduating from Dartmouth that same year. You know, whenever someone says that line about me being the oldest resident, I feel like an antique or something. I never felt like I was old until people started making a big deal about it.

Luckily, my age wasn't a deterrent for landing a job. Actually, I was told all the way through that I would be in high demand because people preferred hiring women who'd already had their babies. In my third year of residency training, I started going through the phone book looking for doctors in the Miami area who practiced internal medicine. I didn't know how else to go about finding a job. My plan was to send out letters saying, "Are you looking for someone to come on with you?"

I had started making a list when I got a call from a friend who said that she'd gone to an exercise class and happened to see a doctor we both knew. My friend mentioned that I was going to be finishing my residency soon and was looking for a job. The doctor said, "Oh really? I thought Linda was going to be staying in academic medicine. Tell her not to accept a position before I talk to her."

So this doctor met me at a restaurant. She told me she was planning to retire. She wasn't that much older than I am—only fifty-eight. But she'd been practicing many years and wanted to spend more time with her husband. She asked me if I wanted to buy her practice.

Talk about things just falling in your lap! Bill and I got her tax statements, saw what she had made over the years and gave them to our accountant. He said, "This is a really good deal if this is what she's been making." So we took out a second mortgage on our house and bought the practice.

It was that easy. This already-made practice just got handed to me—thousands of patients in the middle of Miami Shores, Florida. As an overlap, the other doctor stayed for about six months. For the past three years, it's been just me and my three wonderful medical assistants. The other day I said to them, "Isn't this the greatest?" ✑

JOURNAL ENTRY 2

Twenty-five years ago I gave birth for the first time. In labor, I remember riding each contraction on the back of my breath, all the way up to the crest and down again. Inhale. Exhale. Breath by breath. Time stopped and stretched out. I've spent the last year gestating the idea of this book, locating women to interview and doing research on late blooming. I haven't written a single word.

JOURNAL ENTRY 3

As Linda Bach said the other day, "The hard part is getting started." That certainly has been true in my case. Physicists call this inertia. Objects at rest stay at rest. Objects in motion keep going in the same direction unless acted upon by some outside force. Along this same line of thought, over a year ago I cut out a New York Times *review of the film* You Can Count on Me *by one of my favorite critics, Stephen Holden. In it, he says:*

> ...For all the bullying inspirational slogans hurled at us about never giving up on your dream, following your bliss and today being the first day of the rest of your life, the fact remains that most people's lives run on fairly narrow tracks. And in the real world, as opposed to self-help fantasyland, once you find yourself on a track, it's awfully hard to get off, even if it's headed nowhere in particular....

Fair enough. But it stands to reason that if you do change tracks, then the laws of motion work in your favor.

JOURNAL ENTRY 4

I finished the first chapter last night.

When I began this book, my intention was to have women write their own stories. I imagined a rich symphony of voices and even sent out solicitation letters. But I quickly realized that most of the people I'd selected had neither the time nor the skill to draft a compelling narrative. Reluctantly, I admitted that if I wanted their stories to be told, I'd have to tell them myself. The prospect terrified me.

After procrastinating for months, I started with Linda's because I thought it would be the easiest to structure. Having never written a story before, I didn't know what point of view to take, what style would be best or where to begin.

In my first attempt I tried to imitate a magazine profile piece and, in the process, discovered I don't yet have the verbal virtuosity to do this well. I also decided I didn't want my voice be the dominant one.

Gradually it became clear that I aspire to replicate my experience of sitting with these women in their living rooms and listening to them tell their stories. By some sort of literary alchemy, I hope that others will "hear" their words and, like me, be elementally transformed.

"DON'T BE AFRAID TO TAKE A BIG STEP. YOU CAN'T CROSS A CHASM IN TWO SMALL JUMPS."
—David Lloyd George, English Statesman

IRMA ELDER
ENTREPRENEUR

Born in Mexico, Irma Elder was a teenager when she emigrated with her family to Florida in the 1940s. She didn't speak a word of English. In 1963, she married James Elder and moved to Michigan. They saved their money to buy a Ford franchise, and for the next twenty years Irma stayed home and raised their three children. In 1983 James suddenly died, leaving Irma to take over the business. Accepting the challenge, she became the first woman in Detroit to run an automobile franchise. Today she owns seven dealerships, is on a wide variety of corporate and philanthropic boards, and has evolved from a shy housewife to the CEO of Elder Automotive Group, one of the ten largest Hispanic-owned companies in the nation.

A petite woman with a sweet smile, she's generous with her time and classy to the core. Self-assured, yet genuinely humble, she downplays her success. She'd rather conquer new worlds than rest on her laurels.

Every single person who touches our lives has something to teach us. If we keep our minds open, we can learn from everyone we meet, from the people who sweep the streets to the presidents of corporations. And that's what I've done in my life. I've been like a sponge, learning lessons wherever I go.

I was born in Mexico in a tiny town called Xicotencalt. I'm

told that if you drive by and just close your eyes for a second, you'll miss it. That's how small it is. But when I was a few years old, we moved to Ciudad Victoria, which is where I grew up. Back then, it was already a town of about 100,000 people, but it was still the type of place where everybody knew one another.

I had a wonderful childhood there—not perfect, but wonderful. My mother and father were marvelous people, and I am fortunate to have been born into such a caring family. In the middle of town, my parents had a small dry goods store where they sold pants and shirts and that type of thing.

There were seven children in my family—four girls and three boys—although two of my brothers died. When we were young, a woman we affectionately called Adelita helped take care of us. She told us many stories with moral values that I carry with me to this day.

I still love Mexico, and a few years ago I went back to Ciudad Victoria with two of my sisters and some friends of ours. While we were there, we went to see Adelita, who, by then, was very old. Sadly, I heard that she just recently passed away.

When I was about fourteen, we moved to Miami, where most of our other relatives lived. Coming across the border, I remember seeing children riding their bikes to school, waiting for our train to pass so they could cross to the other side. I had gone to incredibly fine schools in Mexico; but as I looked out the window at these children, I started wondering if going to school in this country would ever be easy for us—if it would ever seem normal.

I went to a Catholic high school in Miami. Because I didn't speak a single word of English, I had to take a couple of steps back and was a year or so older than most of the other students in my class. But the Sisters of St. Joseph were wonderful. During my study periods, one of the nuns would go over the next day's lessons with me.

Besides not speaking English, I also had trouble getting used to the food. My parents were Syrians who had emigrated to Mexico, and we always ate either Syrian or Mexican dishes at home. So I asked my mother every morning to please pack me a lunch, which she did. One day a week, though, she gave me money to buy meatloaf, mashed potatoes and gravy. That was a new meal for me, and I liked it very much. To this day, I love eating those three things.

Don't ask me how, but I acclimated, learned English and became a part of the class. The proof of acceptance came when, after two years in Miami, I was chosen as one of the alternates to go to Girls State in Tallahassee. Two girls were selected to be delegates, and two others were chosen to be alternates. The voting was done by the students and by the teachers, too. I still can't believe they picked me. It was remarkable, really, when you think about it. Most of the students in my class had known each other since first grade and were now juniors in high school. I was just this wide-eyed girl from Mexico. I didn't even quite understand the concept of Girls State.

Then, for some reason, one of the two delegates was not able to go, giving me the chance. I was actually surprised that my parents allowed me to attend, but it was a very interesting experience for me. I learned all about state and local government and the American democratic system. From among the delegates, we chose our own governor and a full Senate and House of Representatives. The wife of one of the Florida senators and the wife of one of the members of the House of Representatives in Washington also came and talked to us. Then on the last night, we had a party with the boys from Boys State, which was nearby.

When we got back to school, the other delegate and I had to give a report. My partner, who was very smart, spoke about the serious part of what we'd learned. It was my job to speak about the social part. I don't know how I expressed myself in my broken English, but I brought down the house. And I learned from this that having a sense of humor is very, very important in life. If you are able to make people laugh, and to laugh at yourself, you are well ahead of the game.

By the time I graduated from high school, I spoke English well enough that I got the highest grade on our English entrance exam for college. Even though my enunciation is not perfect, I do have good grammar. And this goes back to the teachers I had—lay teachers along with the nuns—who inspired and taught me.

After high school, I took a few night classes at the University of Miami, but I don't think that entitles me to say I went to college. I'm the oldest of my sisters and the only one who did not finish college. I've always been a reader, though. Although I don't have much time to read books, I read newspapers and other interesting business and lifestyle publications. I also watch the business news every day to learn and understand what is happening in my industry and others.

Because I come from a very educated family, I have always been very interested in the world around me. My sisters and I used to sit around the dinner table and talk about different topics in the news. We may not agree politically, but we respect each other.

My parents raised us to respect people for who they are. I learned from an early age that if you respect others, they will respect you. For many years, my mother had Christmas dinner at our house in Miami. Anyone we knew who was alone or stranded—from bricklayers to judges and doctors—would come celebrate with us. It didn't matter whether they were Jewish or Agnostic or Catholic or Protestant, or whether they were wealthy or poor. Everyone was welcome. Even after my children were born, we would drive from Michigan to Miami for Christmas dinner. I felt it was so important for them to be part of this caring, hospitable atmosphere.

My parents had a small grocery store in Miami, and I helped out there after I graduated from high school until I secured a position at a tax assessor's office. I worked there a couple of years. Then I was hired as a receptionist at a Chevrolet franchise. I eventually was promoted to secretary to the dealer. He and his wife were wonderful people. He told me that I was the only secretary he ever had that typed with an Hispanic accent. (She laughs.) I was incredibly shy, and he used to love to see me blush. I blushed at almost anything that anybody said.

I was there eight years. Even though I was not directly involved in the business, everything important pertaining to the dealership went across my desk. Consequently, I learned many things that later turned out to be very useful. Once in a great moon when they were short of staff, I would even type a financial statement.

Then in 1963 I met my husband, James Elder, at a Valentine's Day party. He was a sales manager at a dealership in Michigan. We started to date, and within a week he told me that he was going to marry me. I said to him, "I don't think that you know what you're doing. You see me as this nice, sweet girl, and I am nice. But I'm not this sweet person who's just going to bow down to you." I didn't deceive him at all! Six months later, we got married.

My husband was a wonderful man. He was chauvinistic in some ways, not unlike most men of his generation, but he had a tremendous respect for me and my abilities. He immediately put me in charge of the checkbook. I'm very good with numbers and finances —I inherited that from my father—and I paid all the bills. We wanted to buy an auto dealership, so we started a savings plan. In April of '67, we were able to open Troy Ford, located in a northern suburb of Detroit, Michigan—the nation's "auto capital."

The business went through lots of ups and downs. In '73, there was the oil crisis. Then there was an auto strike. Each time we tightened our belts and went on. But then came the '80s, when we experienced the worst recession in the history of the automotive industry. I really admire those dealers who made it. We all had financial concerns. Interest rates were at twenty percent. It was a very, very difficult period. We survived because every penny we had kept the dealership going and our employees employed.

In November of 1983, my husband died suddenly. It was a devastating time in my life. Nothing that has come my way since has compared with the tremendous loss I felt.

The dealership was our only source of income, and I had to decide right away whether to sell or take over the reins. To prove a point, "out of the mouths of babes," I'll tell you a story. One night, my CPA came to the house to discuss some business. Just as he was leaving, my daughter, Stephanie, walked in the door. She said to me, "You look so serious."

I said, "Well, I have to make a decision about whether or not to take over the dealership, and I have to do it soon. I cannot leave a vacuum, otherwise I'll lose the momentum. But if I decide to take over, I'll be competing with other dealers, and they're all men. When I go to meetings, I'll be the only woman. I don't know if I can handle it."

My daughter looked at me and said, "All my life, you've been telling me that I can do anything I want to do. Anything that my brothers do, I can do equally well. It is just up to me. And now you are telling me that you are afraid, that you are only hesitating to become a dealer because you will be dealing with men. If that is the case, then everything you have taught me my whole life has been a lie."

Right then and there I made up my mind that I had to take over the business. I had three children to support, and I wanted to send them through college. My youngest son was twelve, my daughter was sixteen and my oldest son had just turned nineteen. I also needed to save money for retirement, if there was to be such a thing.

On January 1, 1984, I made the leap. It was a big adjustment, but I didn't have time to think about it. I also have to say that the executives at Ford Motor Company were absolutely wonderful. They came to see me after my husband died and asked me what I wanted to do. When I told them I wanted to take over, they didn't discourage me, even though I would be the first woman to own a Ford dealership in the city of Detroit. They wanted me to make it a success.

Of course, not everyone was happy with my decision. After a month, my general manager decided to leave. He ended up taking with him every single one of my salespeople except for two rookies. Eventually, he took my other managers, too. In a few months, almost everyone was gone. How did we survive? When I look back, I think that I was just determined to make it.

But I have to say that it wasn't easy. I faltered, stumbled and fell many, many times. No matter how you describe my leap into the business world, it was not easy. In the beginning I would call my parents and say, "I can't do this." And my father would tell me, "It is not a matter of whether you can do it or not. You have to do it. That's all there is to it. You have to do it for the sake of your kids and for your own sake. So don't give up."

And my mother, who was a very religious woman, would tell me, "I'm saying the rosary for you. It's going to be fine because I'm praying for you." My mom used to say, "The good Lord always takes care of widows and fools," and I'm not sure she didn't think I was both!

I survived by trying to do better each day. After the first general manager left, I found another one, an older gentleman who had retired from the Ford Motor Company. He was very nice, but he had never worked at a dealership before. He didn't stay with me long; but before he left, we had lunch together. He asked me if I would consider selling him the business. "After all, you're only a housewife," he said. I just laughed and told him I didn't want to sell. Deep inside, he believed that women didn't belong in dealerships. And deep inside I knew that we do belong and that we survive long after the criticisms and disbelief in our abilities.

Throughout the years, I have been patronized a lot. But I don't dwell on that. What's the big deal? I'm a big girl. I am very aware of the "glass ceiling" so many executive women experience. I just smile and keep on going. I love being a woman. I would not give up my femininity. I decided early in my career to maintain a feminine appearance with dresses and heels so people would know a woman was in charge. In everything I do, I maintain a low-key approach. You don't have to shout to get your point across.

The only thing that I try never to do, no matter how humiliated I am, or how upset I am, is to cry in front of people at work. Because in this world of ours, people believe crying is a sign of weakness. I don't think it is, but you can't change people's minds. You know the old saying "Laugh and the world laughs with you, cry and you cry alone." This holds true, especially in the business world.

During the twenty years I was a housewife, I learned a lot of skills that came in handy later. I learned how to manage people, how to make a budget, and how to be diplomatic and resilient. Women who stay home are much more capable than people sometimes realize, especially today when so many talented young women are working at home raising their children—participating in school activities and charitable organizations.

I also think that you can't be married to someone for twenty years and not learn something about the business they are in. When my husband was still alive, once a week we had lunch together at the dealership. So I came to know the people there. I also regularly went to the bank with him. When he died, I'd already made all those connections. People knew who I was, and it was easy to communicate with them without having to introduce myself and my intentions.

After I assumed leadership of the dealership, I started going to meetings with other Ford dealers. A few people would leave right afterward, and I would have liked to have left with them because it would have been easier. But I would stay for lunch because I knew that my colleagues would bring up problems they were having, and the others would chime in the discussion. I learned a lot about the business from listening to other dealers.

Then I taught myself how to read financial statements. I spread them out on my family room floor after my children went to bed. I also took advantage of management and related product-knowledge courses that Ford offered. These were very helpful and gave me important insight into the business world and significant information so that I could manage my staff and my bottom line.

I also joined a "20 Group," a group of twenty similar-in-size dealers joined together by the National Automobile Dealers Association (NADA). There are 20 Groups all over the country. My son still belongs to the group I joined years ago. It was a great way for me to keep in contact with other dealers from all over the United States and to share experiences, both positive and negative. We were and are in this business together, and we learned and continue to learn from each other.

A year or so after I took over, I became the dealer principal of Troy Ford. I hired a new general manager. I also hired a new office manager, who was absolutely wonderful. She is still with me. The general manager eventually left and opened his own business, and I was delighted for him. He, too, was with me for several years. I could not have done what I've done without the support and hard world of the people around me.

After we stabilized the dealership, I decided it was time to grow. I attempted to buy some businesses, and each time I tried and didn't succeed, I learned something. I learned how to approach the legal end of the deal, what to ask for and what not to do. I learned very much from my mistakes.

Then I bought Signature Ford-Lincoln-Mercury-Jeep in Owosso, Michigan. This dealership had had three owners in four years. I don't understand what made me think that I should be the fourth owner in the fourth year, and that I would be able to make it work when the other people failed. I had worked hard to make Troy Ford successful; now I thought I could make Signature blossom. It's true that ignorance is blissful.

The biggest lesson I learned from this experience was humility, not to let anything go to my head. Just because I was able to keep the Ford dealership going didn't mean that this would happen every time I took over a business. It was very difficult at first. My son went there for a couple of years to run it and learned a lot, but then we needed him back at the Ford store. Then I sent one of my managers there. He has since become my partner, and now thankfully that business is going very, very well.

Opportunity presents itself in different ways. At the beginning of '92, I met a woman who owned a Jaguar-Saab franchise here in Troy. She was brilliant and had taken over the dealership when her father died. Although she lived in San Francisco, she managed the business and came here once a month. One day we met for lunch, and she asked me if I would like to see her dealership. I'd never been there before, so I said yes. I went over and looked at just the sales area. The cars were beautiful, and the site was on an important dealership avenue in the area. On a whim, I said to her, "If you ever want to sell, please let me know." I really never dreamt that she would sell. I said it almost without thinking.

A couple of months later when she was in Troy again, she telephoned and asked me if I wanted to have dinner with her. I enjoyed her company tremendously and, of course, said yes. At dinner that night I decided that she really wanted to sell the dealership and that she preferred that I purchase it. For nine months we negotiated back and forth, going out to lunch, going out to dinner. If you even say "boo" in Detroit, everyone knows. But we came to an agreement without anyone knowing a thing.

She wanted us to use the same attorney, but I said I couldn't do that. I wanted to find an attorney who was completely impartial and knowledgeable in real estate. I didn't want any conflicts. My sister is an attorney, and she taught me that.

There were two deals: one for the land and one for the business. I presented the land deal without having an appraisal done on the real estate. The woman just told me, "This is what I want." Then I called a friend of mine who was in the real estate business and told him the figure. I said to him, "Well, if my business doesn't work and I have to sell, what would the real estate be worth?" He said, "Well, I might pay you a million less than that amount." And I said, "Okay, if I am only going to lose a million dollars to take this chance, then I'm going to do it."

I am very conservative—always worried about ending up with nothing. I started with very little, and I am still afraid of losing all I've gained. So don't ask me how I got the nerve to do it. I don't know what came over me. I must have had a good feeling about the deal. I rarely go against my instincts.

Once we'd agreed on the basic details, the woman and I worked the "buy and sell" agreements by fax. We spent all day one Saturday and all day one Sunday until we came up with the right agreements. Afterward, I contacted Jaguar. They were a little shocked, but they were fine with me taking over. We have since proven to the company and to our customers that we are serious about our business, our customer service and the manufacturing company we represent. Working hard and having integrity and faith in our capabilities have served my entire family well.

At first we were losing money, so I didn't take a salary. But that was okay. I'm still living in the same house I've lived in for the past twenty-five years. If I had youngsters at home, I'd probably be clipping coupons. In fact, I still enjoy shopping and finding bargains no matter where I travel. Isn't that what I have done all my life? I have negotiated agreements, managed the bottom line, paid attention to saving for the future and re-invested in my business.

Eventually, the Jaguar dealership started to pay for itself, exactly what I wanted and planned for it to do. Troy Ford was also paying for itself, and, with the help of my Owosso partner, so was the Ford-Lincoln-Mercury-Jeep dealership. Then my partner and I opened Signature Ford in Perry, Michigan. This, too, has become a profitable business for the Elder Automotive Group, not just because we purchased it and put our name on the door, but because of the attention to detail, the determination and the shared vision of all concerned.

About three years ago, we changed the name of Troy Ford to Elder Ford. My older son Tony is the president and general manager. We also added an Aston-Martin dealership in Troy and separated Saab from Jaguar and put Saab in its own building. Saab is a wonderful franchise, and the General Motors people have been great to deal with. I have been very fortunate in that respect. The president of Saab USA is a woman and is absolutely phenomenal.

Then we decided to go to Tampa, where we opened a beautiful, state-of-the-art, innovative Jaguar-Aston-Martin franchise. That has been a wonderful experience. My youngest son, Robert, is the president and general manager. My sisters and brother also still live in the greater Miami area, so I like to go there often. While my mother was still living, I bought a house there. Now I do Christmas dinner for everyone, just as she did. Everyone is welcome, and the house is always full of family and friends. When all is said and done, I believe the most important thing in life is your family and your friends.

I also think it's important to give back, so I pledge my time and commit to a lot of charitable boards of directors. I do as much charity work as I physically can. I feel very much for children and the elderly and am especially close to an organization called La Sed. They have a place in southwest Detroit where seniors go for lunch and play games. I am also quite involved with Oakland Family Services. They started a program to train teenage boys how to be good fathers. I commend the individuals who direct these organizations and am proud to be a part of them.

As for my professional affiliations, I recently served on the Chicago branch of the Federal Reserve Board. I was truly amazed that I was asked to be on it. I served two terms, which was the limit, and enjoyed it tremendously, learning and absorbing all I could from the experience. I was also on the board of Lear Corporation, a prominent, publicly-held automotive supplier. They are very honorable business people. Once again, I learned from each of these experiences. When you stop learning, you may as well stop living.

The business world is not something I ever thought I would enter. I used to be very shy and sort of quiet. And even though I'm good with figures, I always thought I would be just a wife and a mom, and that my husband and I would retire and grow old together.

But life sometimes throws you curve balls and gives you opportunities to change. And this is what I did. I never knew I was competitive, but I found out that I was. And it amazed me. When I played cards, I never cared if I won or I lost. What difference does it make? I was really more eager to please the other person than to compete and win myself. But I found out that I enjoy the challenge of making deals and making things happen.

When I first took over the dealership, I thought I was doing it because I needed to support myself and my three children. But I have to tell you that it has become a passion. There are times when I think I must be out of my mind, but I'm in love with the business world. And I'm not done yet. I still have more worlds to conquer. ❧

TODAY, the Elder Automotive Group encompasses Elder Ford, Jaguar of Troy, Michigan (the number one Jaguar dealership in the world in sales of both new and used cars); Jaguar and Aston Martin of Tampa, Florida; Saab of Troy (the number one Saab dealership in the United States in volume of automotive sales); Aston Martin of Troy; Signature Ford-Lincoln-Mercury-Jeep of Owosso, Michigan; and Signature Ford of Perry, Michigan. [P.B.]

JOURNAL ENTRY 5

When I tell people I'm writing about late bloomers, they invariably want to know how I find the women to interview. So far, it's been word-of-mouth. First, I heard about Linda Bach from a mutual acquaintance and traced her through the American Medical Association. Then I heard about Irma Elder from a friend who'd read an article about her in Enterprising Woman *magazine. Although I was nervous about meeting each of these woman face to face, both Linda and Irma were so warm and welcoming that they immediately put me at ease.*

The interview with Linda went without a hitch. I wish I could say the same about my day with Irma. Before I left the dealership, I stopped to check the audiotape of our conversation. I discovered it was broken. My heart began thumping wildly in my chest. I didn't know how much of the interview had been recorded before the tape broke and whether I would be able to repair it. Remembering Irma's rule never to cry in a business situation, I attempted to pull myself together. Then I walked back inside and told her what had happened. She paused for a moment and said, "Let's go back upstairs and do the interview again." That's the kind of woman Irma Elder is.

JOURNAL ENTRY 6

Every morning for the past month I've been reading "Portraits of Grief," a special section of The New York Times *devoted to victims of the September 11th attack. I'm too emotionally drained to do any serious work, and the feel-good tone of my book seems inappropriate right now. But someday soon I need to start writing again. To give up on this book is to give up on myself.*

Dear forty-seven-year-old Prill:

Enjoy yourself more, sweetie. Get a toy box and throw things in it. Read a fairy book. Sing under a bridge. Eat a raspberry sherbet cone. Notice a walking stick. Dress up in a crazy costume. Jump on the bed once in a while. Drink lemonade through a curly straw. Celebrate your birthday with a pink cake. Play, explore—then play some more.

Love,
Eight-year-old Prill

"LIFE SHRINKS OR EXPANDS IN PROPORTION
TO ONE'S COURAGE."   —*Anaïs Nin*

JEAN KELLEY
COLLEGE ADMINISTRATION

Growing up as a poor, physically-abused African American, Jean Kelley left home at fifteen and was pregnant by seventeen. Marrying a man who turned out to be a philandering drug user, she abandoned her dream of going to college and spent two years on welfare. At age forty-nine, she earned a Ph.D. in higher education administration. She recently retired as Director of Student Services at Norwalk Community College in Connecticut.

Tender-hearted and strong-willed, she's tall with large, expressive eyes and a warm, infectious laugh. Making herself comfortable on her living room couch, she takes off her shoes, tucks her legs beneath her and begins to speak in a rich, melodic voice.

I'm not really a late bloomer. I just started so far behind, it's taken me this long to catch up.

My daddy was forty-seven when I was born. My mother was twenty. We traveled by the stars because my daddy couldn't read or write. If he got lost, he wouldn't take out a map like most people do; he'd pull off to the side of the road and look up at the sky. If we were going north, he'd follow the North Star.

Most of my childhood was spent in Smithfield, Virginia, home of the Smithfield ham. Until I was ten years old and my first sister was born, it was just the three of us. We lived in a house that was there since slavery, since God knows when. There was no electricity. No running water. None of those types of things. For water, we went to a stream, although eventually we had a pump. We had a wood stove, and my daddy built an outhouse—a double-seated one with a window. Whoever heard of a window in an outhouse? He was truly creative!

We had an acre of garden—more than enough to feed a family. We had all the vegetables, and we had chickens. At killing time, my father would get extra meats as a bonus from wherever he was working. We didn't have too much store-bought food, but we lived off the fat of the land.

My father farmed for other people. He worked for one person for a long time and then for another. He got paid at the end of the week. Five dollars a day. If the weather was bad, he got nothing. At that time people working at a nearby packing plant were making fifty dollars a week. Twenty-five versus fifty—that's a big difference. Most weeks my father only made fifteen dollars.

Starting when I was about nine or so, I worked every summer with my father in the fields. Growing up, you had to buy books for school. The Smithfield School Board didn't budget money for textbooks, and students were required to buy their own. The higher the grade level, the more books you had to buy, which meant that each year buying books got more and more expensive. My mother didn't work and there was no way on earth that my father with his salary could buy a hundred dollars worth of books. So I weeded peanuts. Weeds grow between the peanuts, and you have to chop them out with a hoe. In the morning I'd take my lunch and set it someplace cool. Then I'd go up and down the rows. Sunup to sundown.

I made four dollars a day. In the summer, you'd mostly get a whole week's work because it didn't rain that much. I was fast. And I always had a job because I was good. I got around two hundred and forty dollars for a summer. A hundred would be for books and another hundred or so would be for clothes.

When I came in from the fields, I had to make dinner. I've been cooking dinner every night since I was six years old. One summer my mother tried to charge me rent. She said, "If you're out there in the fields, then you can't be working in the house. Besides, you're living here and you're eating here. So you've got give some of that back." My daddy told her that it was my money and I should keep it. But if I left it somewhere in the house, my mother would just come and take it. She felt I should pay my way every step.

My mother hated me. Truly she did. She'd beat me, and I'd tell my father. Then he'd fuss at her for hitting me. After he left the house, she'd beat me again because I'd told. If she didn't get a chance to beat me, she wouldn't speak to me for days. I couldn't stand that. That was the psychological part of it.

One time I ran and hid under the house. It was on cinder-blocks. My mother was too big to get underneath, and I thought I'd be safe. But then she went and got a rifle. She said to me, "Get your ass out of there, or I'll shoot you!" She didn't actually fire the gun, but she would have. Years later I learned that she'd been diagnosed with a clinical condition. She wasn't completely right.

So I was in a different world altogether. It seemed like every-one else in Smithfield had TV and indoor plumbing. Meanwhile, my mother was chasing me around and beating me up, and I was out there working in the fields and going to school with books I bought myself.

I loved books, but my mother didn't value reading. I guess she thought it took away from cooking and cleaning. She wouldn't let me use the kerosene, so I waited for the moon to come up to read. My eyes are terrible today. To my mother, bringing books into the house was just like bringing home pornography. So I decided to sneak them in. Hide them somewhere. I put them under my mattress. How would she know? It wasn't as if she would come into my room and clean up. I was the cleaner-upper!

But then one day she did come in and went right to the mattress. She lifted it up and there were my books. Just as she was about to beat me, my father came in. I found out later that daddy had squealed on me. I was maybe fourteen at the time. Anyway, I realized I just wouldn't be telling him things anymore. He was getting older and wanted her love as well as mine. But he also came to save me. He was my hero.

The minister's wife, who was also my fifth grade teacher, was the one who encouraged me to read. She was one of the angels in my life. I went to the Hill Street Baptist Church in Smithfield, and Mrs. Williams was always there. She took an interest in me from an early age. I was smart in school and she liked me. On the weekends, she paid me to clean the parsonage. She gave me clothes and books and got me interested in the classics. She also got me thinking about college. "If you want to go to college," she said, "here are all the books you have to read." One year she even talked to someone and got me a job at the library. I read the whole fiction wall!

Each year more and more of my money went for books until the year I burned myself with the fish. That was the turning point. I was fifteen or sixteen. We had a wood-burning stove, and I had two cast-iron skillets of fish frying with lots of grease in them. Very hot. When you have a wood burning stove, there is a little lifter you use to grab hold of the stovetop and raise it so you can keep putting wood in the fire. You can stick this lifter in the burner when you aren't using it, and that's what I had done. But when I turned around, something of mine caught on it, and one of the pans of fish turned over. I was looking at this and watching the sizzling hot grease roll all down my legs. I knew I was hurting, but I truly wasn't feeling it. I fell down on the floor in shock and screamed. My mom came in and said, "Look what you've done to my floor." She wasn't worried about me. She was worried about the floor! By that time the linoleum was smoking. It had bubbled up with the hot grease.

The accident happened in the morning. We were out in the country, in the woods. There was no doctor. My father helped me up, took me outside and put my leg in a bucket of cold water. I sat there for hours. That's all he could think of to do for me. It was almost sundown before my mother went to get some help. Maybe eight hours later. But she did it. This guy she found took me to the emergency room at Obici Memorial Hospital in Suffolk, which was about twenty miles from where we lived. My right leg was very swollen. It was huge.

I couldn't work that summer. I couldn't even put my leg down; I had to keep it up. Because I couldn't get a job to pay for the books, my mom said, "That's it. You'll have to drop out of school."

I wanted to finish high school and eventually go to college. I couldn't drop out. I just couldn't do that. So I wrote my Aunt Nina in Connecticut. My ace in the hole. I told her what was happening, and two weeks later she was there. She came down. I couldn't believe it. I didn't expect her to come. I expected her to write back. She said, "I got your letter. Let's go."

My mom was so mad. Aunt Nina said I had to make up my mind right then; she was not coming back again. What to do, what to do? My mom said, "When you got burnt, did your daddy get you some help? No! You ungrateful dog!" But if I stayed because I felt sorry for her, then I couldn't go to school. So really, I had to go with Aunt Nina.

I moved to Norwalk, Connecticut, and started tenth grade at Brien MacMahon High School. Folks said I would have a terrible time, that the school was much more advanced than the one I'd been to. But I did fine. I had my own room. I had TV. I didn't even have to cook because Aunt Nina cooked. I helped out, though, and got a part-time job doing housecleaning—a day here and there—in the summers mostly.

We were going along fine until a relative of Aunt Nina's pulled her aside one day and said, "You're letting that girl stay with you and she ain't paying no rent? What's the matter with you?" So Aunt Nina started charging me rent. It wasn't so much the rent per se, but what it told me was that she was my aunt and not my mother. I thought I would be moving there and saving money to go to college—not paying rent. I had even dreamed that Aunt Nina would send me to college herself.

What I found out was that Aunt Nina didn't have much money, although it seemed like she had a lot when she was sending some down South. Fifteen dollars was as much as a whole week's wages. But up North it didn't mean a lot. There was no way she was going to be able to send me to college. Even if she wanted to, she didn't make enough money to send me.

Sure, I knew about scholarships. You go to awards night and get a scholarship for five hundred dollars. Even a thousand dollars. But in the real world, if school costs twenty thousand dollars and you get a scholarship for, say, a thousand dollars, what's that going to do? How're you going to get to college with that? I didn't know about community college back then. Anyhow, my dream was gone. College was over.

So I got another dream. To be somebody's wife. I could cook. I could clean. I was the best housekeeper around. I don't know if this was in front of my mind or in the back of my mind, but that was what I was thinking.

Right around that time, I met my husband at church. One day I was singing in the choir, and afterward one of the other women—the leader, the oldest, the most popular—said to me, "Would you like to come to my house for dinner?" Wow! The in-crowd, you know? Aunt Nina had a rule that I couldn't go out with somebody she didn't know, and she didn't know anybody except the people from the church. So I was in luck.

When I went over to this woman's house, her cousin Bobby was there. She told me that he'd asked her to invite me to dinner. I thought, "Well, isn't that cool?" But actually, that morning he had pointed to the girl standing next to me in the choir and had asked his cousin to invite her, not me. It was all a mistake. I guess Bobby finally told his cousin, but nobody said anything to me. Anyway, Bobby walked me home, and that was the beginning of our relationship. I was sixteen and he was eighteen.

Then I got pregnant. I didn't know I was pregnant at first because I hadn't gone to the doctor and I used to miss my period all the time. But then one day when Aunt Nina and I were on a bus on our way down to Virginia, she asked me if I was. Old people can tell. I thought, "If I am, oh my God, my behind is gone down South again."

So I said to Nina, "I don't know."

"Well, if you haven't been doing nothing, then you know you're not," Nina said.

I was scared to death. We stopped off in Baltimore to see my Aunt Mary, and she got me an appointment with a doctor she knew. The doctor was a gross, nasty man. And, of course, it turned out I was pregnant. I was halfway to Virginia; Bobby was in Connecticut. I was so embarrassed. It was horrible.

Aunt Nina didn't leave me in Virginia. She brought me back to Connecticut. I can't remember if she told my mother I was pregnant. My mother wouldn't talk to me when we visited anyway. She never did. I remember buying Christmas gifts; and the next time I went to Virginia, they were still on the porch, unopened.

As soon as we got back, Aunt Nina called up Bobby and told him to come over. "Okay, what are you going to do?" she asked him.

"Uh...uh...I'm gonna marry her," he mumbled.

"Good answer! Good answer!" Aunt Nina said.

Bobby put a down-payment on a ring, but then he lost his job. It was too late to turn back. Whatever savings I had went into the ring. That should have been my first warning, but sometimes I miss them.

We got married in a little ceremony on October 26, 1968. I had just turned eighteen and was still a senior in high school. I was busy going to school, working and keeping house. I stopped going to regular classes and had a tutor between November and January, when my son was born. Then in February I went back to the regular high school.

Bobby wasn't working, and we needed money. So I got a part-time job at a grocery store. I had all my classes in the morning. Then I'd leave and walk to the store and work there from noon to 8 P.M. After work I'd walk back home. It was a lot of miles. I lost so much weight. I was 5′7″ and I weighed less than a hundred pounds. Can you imagine me being a hundred pounds less than I am now? I couldn't even take a bath because it hurt when I sat in the tub. My head was so heavy, it wobbled! I was working, working, working. But I graduated on time with my class. I cried walking down the aisle.

Six months or so after I graduated from high school, I got pregnant with my daughter. I started thinking, "Why am I working so hard when my husband is sitting at home?" So when I was four months pregnant and could take pregnancy leave, I did.

We needed money, so we took in a girl who was also pregnant and had nowhere to go. We were renting the second floor of a house, along with a finished attic. We gave her the attic. One day I was lying down in the bedroom resting when I heard Bobby and this girl talking. They must have thought I was sleeping.

The girl said to Bobby, "What about her?"

My ears pricked up. I thought they were talking about me.

Bobby said, "Well, I'm going to leave Jean once she has the baby."

I was dumbfounded. As they continued to talk, it came out that Bobby had another woman. Up until then I had no idea that nasty sucker had been cheating on me. I'd noticed, though, that every night at five o'clock—boom—he'd leave. His girlfriend, I later discovered, was working right down the street from our house. Bobby had been going out with her in the evenings after she got home. When I heard him say he was going to stick around until I had the baby, I thought, "Thanks a lot! Don't do me any favors."

As I was listening to this conversation, I was thinking, "What to do? What to do?" First of all, I didn't move. I stayed there on the bed until it was five o'clock and Bobby left. Then I went up to the attic, got a big trunk and put all his stuff in it. I dragged it down to the front porch. His cousin lived downstairs, and her whole family was watching me haul the trunk out of the house. The neighbors were laughing: "She's figured it out!" They knew all along. When Bobby came home that night and found his stuff on the porch, he was so embarrassed he just turned around and walked away.

A couple of days later a welfare lady came to the house because our boarder had applied for assistance. The welfare woman wanted to know how much this girl paid for rent. I told her, "Seventy-five dollars." My rent was a hundred-and-fifty dollars altogether. The woman couldn't believe I was charging seventy-five for a room. I said, "Well, I'm pregnant, I'm not working and my husband just left me. So if she can't pay half, we're both going to be on the street."

The woman said, "You're pregnant? You're probably eligible for assistance."

Right there that day we filled out a form for both of us. I didn't have to go through all the red tape. The other girl had been waiting a while, but it happened just like that for me.

I stayed on welfare for about two years. I hated it. I looked for so many jobs and couldn't get them. Then I'd come home and cry. It would take me a week before I could go out and look again. I interviewed with a woman at a magazine company. She asked me how I was planning to get to work. (I'm not even sure you can ask a question like that anymore.) There was no city bus back then and I didn't have a car. She couldn't imagine that I could walk to work. But, of course, I could have.

Back then, if you had a baby, you didn't have to try and get a job when you were on welfare until the child reached a certain age. But I wanted to work. I was so ashamed every time I got the welfare check and had to cash it. Eventually I signed up for something called the WIN program, which stands for "Work Incentive Now." It was run by the welfare office. No one pays you. You're working for free. You work someplace and hope they'll hire you afterwards. If after three months they don't, the WIN program sends you somewhere else.

I started working in the business office of Norwalk Community College. It was right down the street from where I lived. They had me doing some filing. Then they saw I could do other things and gave me more and more responsibility. By this time, my daughter was almost two and my son was three and a half. Still I wasn't getting paid and no job had opened up. Finally, the folks from the WIN program called Norwalk and said, "Listen, either you give her a job or she's gone."

Luckily, right around this time, someone in the registrar's office gave notice and a job became available. I was eligible, so I took it. I always say, "I never let a boat pass me by." The saying comes from a church story. There's this man who's a really good Christian. Very faithful. He believes that because he's so good, God won't let anything bad happen to him. One day there's a flood. The waters come and the tide is rising. A man comes by in a boat and offers him a ride. The good Christian says, "No thanks." He doesn't think he needs a ride; he thinks God will take care of him. The water keeps rising and rising, and two more men come by in boats. Each time the good Christian declines a ride. Finally, he drowns. When he gets to heaven, he goes to God and says, Why didn't you help me?"

God replies, "What do you mean? I sent you three boats!"

That's why I try to take advantage of each opportunity that comes my way. It might be something sent especially for me.

So on September 1, 1972, I got on the Norwalk Community College payroll. I started working as a clerk-typist. There was a high turnover of people in the registrar's office. It's a hard place to work. I did every job in there. Finally, I said to myself, "Well if I can't get out of this position, at least I can move someplace less hectic." So, I made a lateral move to admissions. It was much more mellow. I was there maybe a year or so.

Then, the registrar's office needed a secretary. A couple of women had quit because they thought they were going to be typing letters, taking dictation and answering phones. What they got was counter duty. One lasted three days and left. So when I was asked if I wanted the job, I said, "Me? Sure. It's a boat!" This was a big promotion, from clerk-typist to secretary.

The only thing is, I had to pass a shorthand test. You have up to a year to take it, though. And as long as you can take dictation, it doesn't matter how you do it. So I did this thing called rapid writing. It was a lot easier than shorthand. I didn't want to take the course, so I got tapes and practiced along with the TV. I practiced everywhere. You could take the test at the employment office. If you didn't do well, you could take it again. Then at least you knew what to study. So, as soon as I could, I took the test. I passed it the first time.

After I'd been at NCC eight years or so, there was an opening for an administrative assistant in student services. I said, "That's my job. It's meant for me." I had worked my way up. This was a "state-exam" job, and the test was in Hartford. A colleague of mine gave me a ride, and we both took the test. Using my rapid writing, I passed the shorthand with flying colors. A hundred words a minute! I also did well on the written part. But I didn't do so well on typing. It was so cold that my fingers were stiff. The three parts were averaged. For the overall score, I was close to the top, but the woman who drove me got the top score.

I didn't think my score was that important. I had taken other state exams and come out number one and had never even gotten an interview. But when it came time to choose an administrative assistant, the dean announced that he was going to select the person with the highest score. I cried my heart out. My supervisor in the registrar's office said to me, "I've tried everything to get you promoted, but without college, I can't. You have to have at least an associate's degree to get ahead."

I had thought about taking courses a couple of times, but I'd always chickened out. Bobby was home again. I'd kicked him out several times, but kept taking him back. I felt bad having two children and not having a husband. I thought that when you were married, you stayed together. But by this time, he'd become abusive. I was working, and he was doing drugs and partying. For any little thing, he'd beat the hell out of me. So I had this husband who was going to kick my butt if I wasn't home on time in the evening. How could I study for a degree when he was around? In the end, my supervisor let me take a course on my lunch hour.

When I walked into that first class back in 1979—it was a psychology course—I almost cried. Everyone knew the answers; they weren't afraid. They were just out of high school and were joking with each other. I was twenty-nine and hadn't been to school in ten years. But I smoked 'em down!

Along the way, I discovered some shortcuts. First, I found out about the CLEP exams, the College Level Examination Program.

The tests were only twenty-six dollars each. There's a whole list of places you can take them. If you pass, you get college credits. If there's something you know that's in your program, you can see if they have a test for it. I CLEP'd English and got six credits. I CLEP'd literature and got six more.

Then I found out about Experiential Learning Credits. I was enrolled in secretarial studies—now it's called business office technology—and got about fifteen more credits for my office skills, typing and shorthand. I had a year's worth of work without taking a single course. I could see the light at the end of the tunnel.

At first, I was taking one course at lunchtime. Then I started taking two. The courses were an hour and a half each, two days a week. But even though I had more money, there were more expenses. So I got a second job at a bank. I'd work from nine to five at Norwalk. During my lunch hour, I'd have my classes. Then I'd work at the bank from five to nine at night. I'd try and leave Norwalk a little early to get there on time. My kids were in elementary school, and my upstairs neighbor, who could hear everything, would keep an eye on them. After work, I'd come home and cook and help them with their homework and play games with them. From midnight to three in the morning was my homework time. Every night.

Bobby was gone so much he didn't even notice that I was going to school. I remember one day he came in when I was studying. We were on the first floor, but we were high up. He threw my books out the window. When he left, I went right out and got my books and started studying again. Sneaking and studying—that's how it always was with me. If Bobby hadn't been such a partier, I never would have graduated!

The courses themselves were therapeutic. You're living in hell and the only way you can get out is to do something else to take your mind off it. You're so worried about the courses, you aren't thinking about what's going on at home. Taking courses was also good for my self-esteem. I felt wonderful when I did well. It took me about three years to get my associate's degree. I graduated in '83 with a 4.0 average. Once I had that degree, if a job opened up that no one else wanted and that I was qualified for, I would take it.

Right around this time, the assistant director of financial aid position became available. One by one, almost everyone in financial aid had quit. It's not an easy place to work. So I took the job. It's a boat. I can paddle. I'm going! I went from a clerical position to a paraprofessional one. I should have had a bachelor's degree, but I got the job anyway.

I wanted to go on and get a bachelor's degree in General Studies at the Stamford branch of the University of Connecticut. UConn and NCC had an agreement that UConn would accept all NCC credits. The whole two years. Then you could negotiate up to thirty credits more. I was a good negotiator. Getting this degree, though, was no lunch-hour thing. How was I going do this? How was I going pay for it? How was I going to get there? I didn't even have a car.

So this is how I did it. I killed two birds with one stone. Upon the recommendation of my UConn advisor, I took some more courses at Norwalk. I also applied for and got the maximum student loan. Twenty-five hundred dollars. I put that money down on a gray Buick Century Limited. Once I had a car, my world just opened up. Bobby, of course, couldn't wait to get in that car; I didn't even get a chance to drive it off the lot before he took it. But I bought something with that Buick. Because now that Bobby had wheels, he was occupied. He wasn't even thinking about me. I told him, "Just give me the car one night a week." In one night, I could do two classes.

The bachelor's of general studies program is tailor-made for adults. You can do with it what you want. I majored in business and minored in English. It was really cool, a nice balance.

While I was getting this degree, I was still working in financial aid. I did that job for a long time and got some great experience. Finally, the director left. The secretary had quit a long time before this. So who was doing financial aid? Me. There was nobody there but me. I was the secretary. I was the boss. I wanted to be the director, but you had to have a master's degree. This was in 1987 and I'd just gotten my B.A. Still, I was asked to be on the search committee.

In the meantime, another angel came into my life, a man named Luis who also worked at NCC. There's always an angel, you know? One day he came up to the office and said, "Hey, you want to go to lunch?"

I said, "Lunch? Who takes lunch?"

"Come on. Take time for lunch," he said.

So we went to lunch and we were in the car when he said to me, "You're going to apply for the job, aren't you?"

I said, "No."

And he looked at me and said, "Are you going to be a good nigger all your life? You apply for this."

Wow! Wake up!

So after lunch, I went to the dean and said, "Take my name off the search committee. I'm going to apply for the position."

I got the job. People come into your life for a season or a reason, you know? Luis was only at NCC six months. I didn't have the right degree, but I had the equivalent experience. I was no longer a paraprofessional. I was a professional! Big time, big bucks—at least for me.

Just recently, I saw Luis at a professional development day and told him that story. He said, "Oh that was nothing." But if it hadn't been for him, I wouldn't be where I am today.

By this time things were horrible with Bobby. He was strung out on drugs. He had lost weight and was really thin and was taking my money and taking my car. One night, my friend Louise called me on the phone, and I was talking to her when Bobby came in. He must have thought I was talking to my colleague Luis, not my girlfriend Louise. And just like my mom used to do, he came up behind me and hit me. He knocked my glasses off and the phone out of my hand. I screamed. The kids were teenagers at this point, and they ran into the room. My son came flying around the corner and slammed something into his father's face. Then my daughter jumped in. My babies were fighting for me! I couldn't let them fight alone, so I joined them. The three of us were on top of Bobby.

Bobby looked up and said to my son, "I can't believe you are doing this. I'm going to kill you. You are dead!"

My daughter and I screamed. Together, we held Bobby down. My son ran out of the apartment, but we couldn't hold Bobby down forever. What to do? What to do? I had to make a decision quick.

I said to my daughter, "Okay, you run next."

She said, "Nope. I'm not leaving without you. You run."

I said, "No, you run."

If Bobby hadn't been on drugs, I think he would have gotten up and killed us both before then. So anyway, I don't know how Bobby got up, but he flung me one way and my daughter the other. I knew he had a gun in the house and I thought he was going to get it. I said to myself, "I've stayed in this so long, and now he is going to go kill my son. If God lets me out of this, I will never, ever, ever let that man back in my house."

It was a crazy mess. My daughter and I ran to Norwalk Hospital. We didn't live far from there. It was winter, and I didn't have any shoes on. My feet were so cold that I thought they were going to fall off. In the meantime, Louise had called the police. They came and arrested Bobby. He said, "How can you arrest me? They jumped me. I want to have them arrested." But we were the ones who were battered and bruised, so the police put him in jail.

I got my kids back. I got my car back. I got my dog back. Then I got my stuff and left. We went to my cousin's in Stamford. By that time no one in the world could stand Bobby. Nobody would bail him out, so he stayed in jail a long time. The very next week I got a lawyer and started divorce proceedings. We'd been married nineteen years. The total, total end to our relationship came when I bought my condo. Bobby couldn't get back and forth to Bridgeport, which was a couple of towns away from Norwalk.

After Bobby went to jail, I stayed as the director of financial aid for ten years, from 1987 to 1997. During that time, I went back to get my master's degree at Southern Connecticut State University. I had to drive to New Haven. I would get out of work at four and be in class by five. My M.A. was in urban education. I always had trouble figuring out what to major in. I chose what would get me through the quickest.

If you have a master's degree, it doesn't matter what it's in. I'd been to a lot of meetings as director of financial aid, and everyone had a master's. I was embarrassed that I didn't. I just hadn't had the opportunity. If I have an opportunity to do something, I can do it. I finished my master's degree in '94. Ironically, my son also graduated from Southern. For a year, we even overlapped and sometimes bumped into each other on campus.

I hadn't thought about getting a Ph.D., but the dean put the idea in my head. I thought, "Well, where?" I went up to Storrs, where the University of Connecticut's main campus is, and felt at home there. I applied to its Ph.D. program in higher education administration.

Again, I got student loans. Working in financial aid, I knew that as a graduate student, I could get eighteen thousand a year. I also discovered that at UConn, courses are cheaper in the summer. You can save big time. At one point, they were even cheaper than

Norwalk!

Then I applied for a sabbatical from work. I figured, what do I have to lose? I got it. I was still the director of financial aid, but the president asked the assistant director of financial aid and the financial aid counselor whether they would cover for me. They both said, "Sure." Really nice people. For no extra money or anything, they covered for me for six months.

So, for the first time in my adult life, I was a full-time student. This was the spring of 1996. Full-time was nine credits, but it didn't cost more to add credits. So I did fifteen. Even if you take one course at a time, you're going somewhere.

Finally, I could do research in the library, spend time in the computer lab and have dinner in the cafeteria like a real student. My kids were now grown up, so I could even come home at midnight. Before I went back to Norwalk, I got six more credits. By that time, I had twenty-one altogether. You only need fifty-four to graduate, so I was well on my way.

Someone at that time asked me why I didn't use my sabbatical to do my dissertation, like most people do. But with all that traveling—UConn is exactly a hundred miles from NCC—I needed my sabbatical to do my course work. I could do my dissertation at night or take some vacation time. I had lots of vacation time by then.

For my dissertation, I wanted to do something that I was excited about. Being in financial aid, I had access to all the financial aid data and to all sorts of community college data. The hot topic of the day was retention. So I put that all together and decided to look at what factors were the most important for student retention in the community college population.

After I'd done all the research and my dissertation proposal had been approved, I went out and bought SPSS, a program for social science majors to do statistical analysis. I didn't know how to use the program at first, but I played with it. So I entered all my data, played with all these statistics and wrote it up. That was that. I love to tinker!

My dissertation was more than two hundred pages. I was so excited about it. I knew the population. I knew the people. Number 34? I know him! Wow! Interesting! For my oral defense, I did a PowerPoint presentation. I got a big conference room. It was impressive just to walk in there. I used everything—a monitor, a big screen. I'm not a public speaking kind of person. I don't do that very well. But I had lived this and loved it, and I could speak about what I knew. After I finished, I was out of the room less than a minute before my advisor came back to get me. "Congratulations! You did it!" he said. It was that smooth. I got my Ph.D. on October 27, 1999. I was forty-nine years old.

After I finished my courses, but before I completed my dissertation, one of the deans asked me if I would be interested in tinkering with some expensive software the school had bought for the career center. The program was just sitting on the shelf. She knew that I'd been looking to branch out and do something different and that I'd been playing with all this financial aid software for my research. She thought I'd be the perfect person to get the program up and running. But I didn't have the time. How could I do that when I was still doing financial aid?

Right around this time, though, the director of student services retired. The president, seeing an opportunity, announced that anyone with an idea for reorganizing the department should write up a proposal. He said that not only would he read these proposals but he'd also meet with the people who wrote them. That's how I got to talk to him. I had a totally different proposal than the one he used, but it got me an audience. I said to him, "I can do so many things. I'll do anything." He made me the acting director of student services and put financial aid under me.

It was a promotion. I was so excited. What I secretly wanted, though, was to be dean of students. The dean of students reports only to the president. People get those positions and then stay there and die. The dean wasn't sick, but then she surprised everyone by announcing she was going to step down. I thought God sent this for me. This is it. My dream. I did my resume. I got an interview. I was a finalist. Then one afternoon, the president came to me and said, "It's close, but we feel that your competition has an edge over you. We're going to give her the job." I thanked him for coming over and cried for about a month.

I almost lost my mind. I was thinking to myself, "I've worked my way through school, sneaking around to study. I've worked for the college for free. I've done everything. How could this person have an edge over me? What more could I have done?" For four months, I lost it. No one knew. Every day I worked as hard as I could. But I cried myself to sleep every night. I don't think I'll ever hurt that way again. Oh God! What did I do wrong?

In 1998 I applied for and became the official director of student services. I was no longer just acting. By that time I was out of tears anyway. I had a job that paid a nice salary. I had tenure. I had freedom. Most of all, I had two wonderful children and great friends who'd been by my side all these years. "What are you crying about?" I asked myself.

Then, in the summer of 2001, I was suddenly given the opportunity to be the interim dean of students at Housatonic Community College, right near where I live. The HCC job had opened up earlier and I'd applied, but I didn't even get an interview. In the meantime, the person they'd hired hadn't worked out, so there was an opening again. I couldn't believe it. Of course, I took the job. This wasn't some little boat. I thought this was a ship sent especially for me.

As it turned out, I wasn't selected for the permanent position. I was the dean of students for one semester only. On my last day at Housatonic, there was a big party in the conference room. People from all over the college came. We partied until two in the afternoon, and then we went to lunch.

Afterward, I came back to the office and stayed until closing time. At five o'clock, I turned off the computer, switched off the lights and walked away. That was it. I said to God, "Okay. What's next? I'm ready." ✍

AFTER JEAN LEFT HOUSATONIC, she was welcomed back to Norwalk Community College as its director of student services. She retired in the spring of 2003. In an e-mail dated January 30, 2004, she writes: "I am traveling, reading and doing all the things I enjoy. I am even exploring options for a possible second career. My life now is like a dream come true. I wonder what I ever did to deserve all this happiness." [P.B.]

The other day when I started to transcribe the three tapes from my interview with Jean Kelley, I discovered, to my horror, that the first one was almost entirely blank. Putting herself through elementary school, being shot at by her mother, living with Aunt Nina—all that was gone. I felt as though I'd lost some priceless treasure that a dear friend had entrusted to me. "How could I have done this again?" I kept asking myself. "I must be an idiot!"

Too embarrassed to call Jean and tell her what had happened, I e-mailed her at Housatonic Community College. A day went by. No word from her. I thought, "Oh God, she thinks I'm a fool. She'll never talk with me again." (As my friend Harry Schneider once gently pointed out to me, I automatically go to the darkest place inside and assume the absolute worst when I think I've done something wrong.)

Then yesterday I had lunch with someone who used to work with Jean. (We'd planned the date weeks in advance.) As we were waiting for our meals, my friend casually mentioned that Jean wasn't selected for the permanent dean of students position. I was shocked. In my mind, she was the perfect person for the job. My friend agreed. Then it dawned on me: My letter to Jean had ended up in e-mail limbo. She'd never received it.

So last night I mustered up my courage and dialed her number. She was elated to hear my voice. It turns out she'd been trying to get in touch with me, but had misplaced my e-mail address and phone number. She'd been wanting to break the news that she was no longer at Housatonic.

In the course of our conversation, she also said that sharing her story last fall had been surprisingly therapeutic. Until we talked, she didn't quite realize how much grace she'd experienced and how much she'd accomplished. Getting some distance on her life and seeing it whole had given her a sense of peace.

We're going to get together again in a few weeks. This time I'll check twice to see if I've turned on the tape recorder. But on another level, it strikes me that perhaps those things we think of as mistakes aren't really mistakes at all.

JOURNAL ENTRY 9

A powerful moment today. Driving up my street this morning, I began wondering how and where I would find my next person to interview. Just as I pulled in the driveway, Jo Fuchs Luscombe, who lives next door, was pulling out. We both stopped to say hi, and I started telling her about my book. She lit up and said, "I'm a late bloomer. Maybe you should interview me."

"YOU HAVE WITHIN YOU MORE RESOURCES
OF ENERGY THAN HAVE EVER BEEN TAPPED,
MORE TALENT THAN HAS EVER BEEN
EXPLOITED, MORE STRENGTH THAN HAS EVER
BEEN TESTED, AND MORE TO GIVE THAN YOU
HAVE EVER BEEN GIVEN."
—John Gardner, founder of Common Cause

JO FUCHS LUSCOMBE
FORMER STATE
REPRESENTATIVE

Staying home to raise her two children, Jo Fuchs Luscombe didn't venture into local politics until she was divorced and in her forties. Then, at age forty-eight, she ran for and won a seat in the Connecticut House of Representatives. Eight years later, she became Republican Minority Whip. Today, she is remarried and still active in community affairs.

Standing barely 5´2˝, her hair styled in a pageboy, she could easily slip under the radar. But she's as savvy as she is smart, and unafraid to speak her mind. She's a Texas-style steel magnolia.

From an early age my mother, who is a wonderful woman, instilled in me an understanding that it is important for those who have to extend a hand to those who do not.

I was born in Dallas, Texas, and was a skinny, shy little gal. My father, a real Texas hell-raiser and lifelong Democrat, worked for a subsidiary of Gulf Oil. When I was a year-and-a-half, we moved to Venezuela. We lived there sixteen years.

In Venezuela, many cultures live side by side: Indians, Europeans, Africans and, of course, Spaniards. As a consequence, I grew up speaking both Spanish and English. Zoning was nonexistent. A lovely, comfortable home could be right next door to squalor. Hardly a day passed when someone didn't come by our house asking for money, food or clothing. My mother never turned anyone away.

At one point we lived in a Spanish-style house. Next door was a big family. Thinking back, their home was probably not on par with ours, but at the time I was just aware that it was small compared to what we had and that it had to house considerably more people.

The family had a little girl named Ana Maria who was about my age and very sweet, very shy. Ana Maria often stood outside in the courtyard and looked up at our house. If I was at the window, she would have this sad smile on her face and would sometimes wave at me. I took to dropping sweets out the window to her, and she would rush to pick them up. It got to the point where I would be running around looking for anything I could find to drop out the window. My mother, who didn't want Ana Maria's family to think we were giving them charity, asked her mother if she objected. The mother was very gracious and said she didn't mind. She was aware I was doing this and aware that it was giving both her daughter and me pleasure.

I also remember riding a school bus with my brothers and sisters—I'm the oldest of six—and passing several poor communities on the way to school. Children would stand on the side of the road and wave to the yellow bus, and we would wave back. To this day, I'm not certain if these children even went to school. All of us on the bus had little lunch pails, and we started saving part of our lunches to share with these kids. The bus driver was so enchanted with this that he would slow down so that we could lean out the window and let the children grab the food as we were driving by.

I began giving so much of my lunch out the window of the bus that my teacher became concerned that I wasn't eating sufficiently. She talked to my mother, who subsequently got to the bottom of what was going on. My mother then started making me two sandwiches, with the understanding that I was to eat one and share the other.

Sharing made me feel wonderful. I think it was just the idea of giving somebody else joy. These kids on the side of the road looked forward to getting something from the kids in the yellow school bus. It had serious overtones, but I suspect at that tender age it was just a game. At any rate, these experiences certainly turned me in the direction of knowing that there is great need in the world. All I had to do was open my door and look outside.

The oil camp schools only went through ninth grade; so for high school, my parents sent me to a boarding school in Texas. After I graduated, I stayed in Texas and attended a small college in San Marcos. I also went to Katharine Gibbs School, where I learned office management skills. I always tout Katharine Gibbs.

When I was nineteen, I married an oilman, which is not so surprising considering my life was the oil industry. I was a mother by twenty. In those days, oil companies looked after their employees, and employees developed great loyalties to the companies that hired them. We always had that big umbrella over us.

Early in our marriage, we moved to Libya and stayed for five years. The Arabic language was a bit hard for me to master, but Italian was the second language in those days. (The Italians had colonized Libya in 1911.) It was easy for me to learn Italian because it is so similar to Spanish; and since I could communicate, I was able to do very well.

We lived there in the early- to mid-sixties. Libya was racing to catch up with the rest of the world. Oil had been discovered, and American companies were coming in droves. At that time Libya also housed the largest American airbase outside the United States —in Tripoli. The country was a kingdom then, and King Idris was a progressive-thinking individual. He knew that there would have to be change. It was happening gradually, but it was happening. You could see women behind their veils and men with their loads being carried by donkeys and just imagine being back in

Biblical times. But now, the country suddenly had money and reform was taking place. On the other hand, there were fundamentalists who resented fast change and who wanted religion to play a major role. In 1969, the king was toppled by a military coup. We had left just before that.

My experiences in both Venezuela and Libya gave me an enormous respect for getting along with people and trying to understand them. Every country has its own culture that dictates how one thinks and how one behaves. Other people's way of doing things isn't necessarily our way of doing things. It always concerns me that we Americans think so highly of our ability to get things done. We have a great deal at our disposal. A lot of countries don't have those resources and opportunities. So it really is important for us to be sensitive to their situations as well as to their needs and wishes.

When my husband's job was done in Libya, there was the possibility of our moving to Nigeria. But we decided not to go, mainly because by then we had two little boys. Wanting the children to start school in America, we returned to the United States.

At first, we settled in the Washington, D.C., area. But then in 1969, for business reasons, we relocated to Westport, Connecticut. The boys were around ten and thirteen when we moved to New England. Up until this time, I was a devoted mother and the wife-that-helped-the-husband. I made sure the kids' diets were right, their doctors' appointments were kept, their teeth were brushed. I watched their games and took them where they needed to go. I wasn't the head of anything. I baked cookies for PTA bake sales and did church work. That was about it.

Then, when I was in my mid-thirties, my husband and I were divorced. We could both see it coming. Finally, one day my husband said we had to face up to this. We realized that we had grown in different directions and that our needs were different. The marriage just wasn't working. Today I can tell you without any hesitation that it takes two to tango.

My husband traveled a great deal with his job, so for a long time we were able to keep from the children the fact that we were not getting along. We probably did them a disservice, not letting them in on it early, because they were heartbroken when the split came. My friends were as shocked as my kids because I had really not shared with them either. I just felt that my troubles were my own, that my unhappiness was a private thing. Now when I'm not happy, I'm an open book.

Everyone around me was very concerned about what this was going to mean. Would I be able to stay here? How would I cope? What would I do? Fortunately, I didn't have financial problems because my husband was generous. I'm not saying I was rich by any stretch of the imagination, but I had a roof over my head and food on the table. I was also able to keep the house, which was in my name. I've had occasion to come in contact with women who have gone through divorces and were in far worse situations than I was, primarily because of money but also because they were simply not prepared to go it alone. I have one friend who suffered a serious breakdown after a divorce because she had never even written a check.

This was probably the saddest time of my life. No one likes to think that they have failed. The divorce was also very painful for me because I knew a breakup would mean that the boys would have divided loyalties. That probably bothered me more than anything. I also knew that whatever I chose to do in the future, I would have to do it alone. I had never had that experience. I went from being a sheltered daughter to a sheltered wife—always with a company umbrella over me. When the marriage ended, I knew that I had two routes I could take. I could either wallow in self-pity and do nothing with myself, or I could pick up the ball and run. I did the latter.

My former minister, the Reverend Dana Kennedy, always says that I got my political beginnings at Christ and Holy Trinity Church. I suppose that's true. The first thing I did when I moved to Westport was to join the church. I thought it was important for the children to have a religious education. When Reverend Kennedy came to call for his first visit, he tried to bring me out, to find out what my interests were and how the church could fill any void in my life. He also mentioned several areas where I might be of help. He wasted no time in signing me up.

The church in those days had genuine needs, and I was immediately made to feel welcome. I eventually headed up everything there was to head up. I was president of the Women's Guild. I was on the Vestry. I ran the fundraisers. It wasn't that I looked to be the head of things; it just turned out that way.

In addition to the church, early on I got involved with the Westport Historical Society. Along with some other ladies, I became concerned that there wasn't a centrally-located permanent home for the organization. We zeroed in on a house that was owned by my church. The house needed a lot of work, and Christ and Holy Trinity had no real use for it, so the church agreed to sell it to the Historical Society.

When I was asked to consider being part of a team that would go out and look for the funds, my first reaction was to say, "I don't know anything about fundraising." My fundraising had been limited to cake walks for the PTA. But I said yes; and the next thing I knew, I was one of three women raising the needed money. I don't think any of us had ever done serious fundraising before. We were all young, inexperienced, naïve. But I'm so glad I did it. Throughout the years I've really perfected my fundraising skills.

You also have to remember that this was a time when women were coming into their own. There was a lot about this in the papers, in the magazines, on television. And Westport was a town in those days where the men commuted out and the town was left for the women to run. There is such a thing as being in the right place at the right time, just as there is something to be said for knowing the right people. And a little bit of both of those things have played into my life.

My political career began at a ladies' luncheon. I was at The Three Bears Restaurant in Westport, sitting next to a woman who was on the town's Zoning Board of Appeals. She got to telling the group about her role as a member of the board. I made a casual comment like, "Gee, that sounds interesting," and she turned to me and said, "We have an opening. Would you like to interview for it?"

Running for elective office was the furthest thing from my mind. I wasn't sure how to answer. Then she said, "Well, I'll tell you what. Why don't you come to our hearing tomorrow night and size us up?" So I went. I thought, "I can do this." I filled out someone's unexpired term, just short of two years. That was in 1980. I was forty-four years old.

When the term ended, I had to run on my own right. By that time, though, I knew exactly what the job entailed and how to structure a campaign. Our terms were staggered, and I had been watching other board members run. I ran against a doctor, who happened to be a very tall, fine gentlemen. There are definite disadvantages to being short, and my supporters were worried sick that it would work against me. But it didn't.

Running for office was a little scary. I was out on a limb for everyone to look at, to support or not to support. But my friends all came forward and helped. Without them, I couldn't have done it.

In those days, I was not a great public speaker. I dreaded the speeches I would be called upon to make. Even now, I'm better at speaking off the cuff than I am at prepared speeches. Back then, though, my hands would get clammy and I'd get these little butterflies in my stomach and I'd think, "Oh God, I am going to be awful." I should have gone to Toastmasters. It probably would have improved my ability and saved a lot of wear and tear on the nerves. But somehow or other, even though I still get nervous when making speeches, I overcame all of that. There's nothing like practice.

The first speech I gave was before the Westport League of Women Voters. My opponent—the tall doctor—was going to be there. We were given a subject and told to speak about ten minutes. I can remember getting up there and just feeling like I was going to throw up. But I survived. Afterward, I was told that I wasn't at all bad. The doctor, I am sure, was better, but it didn't matter because not that many people showed up anyway.

Despite the fact that I was short and not a doctor, I won. I ran as a Republican and was elected to do a four-year stint in my own right. (I'm really not a partisan person, but it is important to affiliate with a party for a number of reasons.) Two years later I was chairing the board and leading the meetings. I did a total of almost six years on the zoning board. As far as elective office goes, this was considered low-rung. But it was a wonderful experience.

Even though I sort of backed into politics, by this time I'd gotten the bug. The truth is, once you learn how to deal with people and run things, you can expand on that. It's easy to go from one job to another. After I'd been on the zoning board for five years, I had become fairly well known among the political circle, and folks started thinking of me in other roles because they knew I would inevitably tire of being on the board. So I was constantly being asked whether I would consider running for this or that.

Eventually, there was a race for First Selectman. In Westport, the person who loses the First Selectman's race becomes the

Third Selectman, but the person who lost refused to serve. So the First Selectman who won the race appointed me and I served out the term.

In 1986, at the same time I was serving on the Board of Selectmen, my good friend, Julie Belaga, who was the State Representative for our district, decided to run for governor against Democratic incumbent Bill O'Neill. Of course, Westport was thrilled that they might have a hometown girl as governor. There were also many of us excited about having a woman, and we all got behind the campaign.

Julie's finance chairman raised a fast thirty thousand dollars, but he was a tremendously busy man. Mike Belaga, Julie's husband, remembered my fundraising experience with the Historical Society and asked me if I would consider taking over the position. It was an enormous job, but I accepted.

I raised a quarter of a million dollars for Julie's campaign. To do this, I had to travel all over the state. On one trip, I went with a friend to Hartford to collect a check from someone who was going to give what we considered a generous contribution. It was the end of the workday, and after I collected the check, my friend went to retrieve his car. I was waiting on the steps of a shopping complex in the rain with my umbrella. The check was in my pocketbook. Then I saw this gentleman. I don't know what made me notice him in particular. He was nicely dressed and looked very personable. As he walked toward me, I had the sense that he was going to stop and ask me for directions and that I wasn't going to be able to give them to him. I was in downtown Hartford; that's all I knew. I was lucky that I got there at all.

Anyway, he stopped in front of me and smiled and said, "I'll take your money." Just like that. There were people all around, hurrying home. No one was paying attention. I think I had all of about twenty-three dollars on me. I was wearing a diamond ring.

I had a gold chain and a gold bracelet. He could have taken anything he wanted.

I said to him, "I don't have very much on me."

And he replied, "I'll take what you have." I handed over the twenty-three dollars. He took it, said "thank you" and walked away into the crowd.

I was stupefied. My legs were like jelly. Then he stopped at the corner, turned around and started to come toward me again. I couldn't find a voice to scream. I just stood there.

When he reached me, he said, "You really shouldn't be where you're standing. It's not safe. Didn't your mother ever tell you not to stand on street corners? Now you walk over there under that light. You'll be safe there."

It was all I could do to make my legs move, but I did it. I stood under the light post, and he disappeared again. He just walked away. That was my first experience with Hartford. It's a wonder I ever returned.

I didn't realize it at the time, but a little over a year later I would be there in my own right. What happened is that one day Julie came into her headquarters and said to me, "Have you given any thought to running for my seat? I think you would be quite well suited for the job, and I am not going to be running for it again. You should really think about it, Jo."

I did, and decided to go for it. It was a natural progression, from the local to the state. I had done seven years of elective office in Westport. Still, this was a major leap.

First, I had to run in a primary because somebody else wanted the job. I don't think you ever get a hundred percent used to campaigning. But you know when you go into it that you are either going to win or lose and that you will have to do many things to promote yourself. Some of it was rather foreign to me. You have to be everywhere, pressing the flesh, as they say. Going door-to-door you sometimes see people that you know, and you have to develop an art because you can't get bogged down too long talking to one person. There are also times when people are not so amenable to having you. One time I rang someone's bell. No answer. But there was a car in the driveway, so I thought, well, I'll try once more. A window opened upstairs and a woman leaned out and said, "I don't answer my door to strangers, and neither should you."

I survived the primary, but then I faced a very significant opponent in the real race. She had been married to an attorney, an important individual who had died at an early age. It was almost like running against him. It was my toughest, closest race, but I pulled it off.

The first time I drove into Hartford after the election, I remember the beautiful gold dome of the capitol building coming into view and thinking to myself, "That's my house." In the life of any legislator, I think there is that feeling of "I got here; I made it." And there was always, at least with me, a sense of awe. I never lost that. Even if I went in every day, there would be this magnificent building in front of me, and I would think to myself, "I am part of this!"

I became consumed with the job. I wanted to be good at it. It was a learning curve, too, and I enjoyed that part. I found gratification in almost everything I was able to do. You do make a difference. There are no two ways about it. More than anything, I liked being in a position to help others. I got to know people in powerful jobs, and a telephone call from me to a commissioner could just cut right through the red tape.

One young woman here in town had lost her husband. While on vacation, he had rented a plane, gone out to fly and never come back. She was left with a very young child—under a year old at the time. The law is such that if there is no body, no evidence of a wreckage, you have to wait seven years to get Social Security.

She was frantic. She couldn't afford day care, so she couldn't go to work. She was trying to get Social Security Disability, but she couldn't get past the law. She needed help. Social Security is federal, not state, but there is a state office in Hartford. So I called it and found out what to do. Then I took her and sat with her while she went through all the formalities to get benefits. Today, we are still friends. She completed her education, her little girl is now in middle school, and she has a business she runs out of her home. She really pulled herself up. So that was a wonderful, wonderful experience for me.

There was another man who had suffered a very serious heart attack, and his doctor said he couldn't work. He was young, probably in his mid-forties, when this happened, and he was totally incapacitated. He had no income, and he had a family to worry about. He was trying to get Disability and was getting the runaround. So I called my congressman, Chris Shays, whom I knew personally from our years together in the House, and said, "This guy needs help." Chris stepped right in and cleared the deck. Today this gentleman's health has improved. He's holding down a job. His wife also got a job. But for a long time he needed those Social Security payments, and I was delighted to be able to help. I loved doing constituent work.

I was also happy doing the small, daily things. With every piece of legislation that came before me, I had to think: How is this going to affect the district that elected me? And very often that was different from how it was going to affect other parts of the state. So I had to specifically think about the area that I represented, but in general terms I had to keep the state in mind. The needs of some of the surrounding cities and towns are greater than Westport's. Sometimes I had to let my conscience and my heart dictate what I did, even though it wasn't what my district needed.

In the legislature I honed those consensus-building skills I'd learned years before on the zoning board. Hundreds of pieces of legislation come before you in any given year, and you know that no two people are going to look at the proposals in the same light. Often the need exists to arrive at a compromise.

In my second year, I was promoted to leadership. For the next six years, I was an assistant minority leader of the House. I think one of the reasons I was promoted so quickly was because I was more mature. I had had more life experience. Many of the legislators were extremely bright, but they were young.

In my sixth year, district lines were redrawn. Whereas before I had all of Westport, now I had half of the town and a portion of the city of Norwalk. I was worried about running in this new district, but what helped me enormously was that Norwalk has a very large Hispanic and Italian population and, of course, I speak Spanish and Italian. I also had a young man who volunteered to help me in Norwalk who was half Italian, half Greek and spoke both languages. We would go to a house and try and guess whether the occupants spoke Italian, Greek or Spanish. When you can speak to someone in his own tongue, you have a leg up. This gentleman's family also owned a seafood restaurant that used to be right on the water in Norwalk, and he introduced me to a lot of people in town. So I was fortunate. I was able to keep my seat. For my last two terms in the legislature I represented this new district.

The final thing that happened was that I became Republican Minority Whip of the House. The Speaker controls what bills come up for a vote, and the major role of the whip is to make certain that you know at any given time what kind of votes you have on your side. Again, it was one of those things that evolved. By the time you've been there eight years, you know how the game is played. You know the players. The players know you.

In 1987 I was sworn in, and in 1997 I went out. In the back of my mind, I felt like one should leave on top, that one shouldn't

wait to be voted out of office. What finally triggered my departure was that I was in the chamber one day and all of a sudden this
young, very new legislator stood up—he was from the northern
part of the state and cute as a button—and introduced a bill I had
introduced nine years before. I thought to myself, it's time to go.
By the way, he didn't have any more success with the bill than I
did. (She laughs.)

When the ten years ended, I was casting about, not completely
certain what I was going to do. Then the head of the Westport
Representative Town Meeting called and asked me to consider
interviewing for the School Building Committee. I thought it was
an important job and that not many people would want to do it
because it would probably be controversial. It would cost money,
the taxpayers wouldn't be happy, and so on. I asked a number of
people what they thought, and everyone said I shouldn't do it. But
a couple of days later I called back and said I would on the condition that the interview could wait until I got back from some trips
I'd planned.

Months before I had signed up for a tour to England, Scotland
and Wales. Then my son, who lives in Singapore, called and said,
"Why don't you come for the Chinese New Year?" I thought,
"Why not do both? How often do your kids call you up and want
you to visit?" I spent two weeks with my son and had a wonderful
time. It was just the grandest experience. Then I came back to
Westport and left a few days later for Europe. I met my husband,
John, on this tour. And, of course, my life changed completely.
This was in 1997.

When I returned from my travels, I interviewed for the School
Building Committee, which I have now chaired for the past five
years and which has overseen five major building projects. It has
kept me very busy and has made me deal with significant town

issues. I also met a whole segment of the Westport population that I would never have met. I am dealing with young people who have young kids, which keeps me thinking young and abreast of what is important in their lives. I would have missed that altogether.

To this day, I'm active in a lot of organizations. The ones I gravitate toward are those that help others to help themselves. I'm also a grandmother four times over. One of my sons is fond of saying to me, "Whatever happened to the old-fashioned grandmother that sat in her rocking chair and baked cookies?"

And I say to him, "Oh some of them are still around, but I'm not one of them."

I think those women who are content to stay home should not feel diminished in any way. For a lot of years, my kids were the most significant thing in my life. Now I'm doing my thing. Retiring is not my style. ✍

JOURNAL ENTRY 10

I'm struggling with doubt. The trick, I suspect, is to turn away before it grabs you by the throat. My personal demon sits on my shoulder wearing a gray business suit and a fedora and whispers in my ear that I'd better keep my day job. "You're not a writer," it taunts me. When I shared this with my mom, she remarked, "That little devil sounds just like your dad!"

JOURNAL ENTRY 11

My father was a warm, funny, brilliant and generous man and I know he loved me. The fruits of his hard work and subsequent success have rippled outward across time and space and given me the freedom to quit my teaching job to write this book. He lived large and inspired me to follow in his oversized footsteps. I have only gratitude for being his daughter.

That said, my father was also a volatile alcoholic and a tremendously insecure man. He berated and belittled and terrorized me. And he told me I was stupid so many times and his words penetrated so deeply that, even after graduating Phi Beta Kappa from Georgetown and writing this book, I still believe what he said. I know now that this feeling may never completely disappear, no matter what I accomplish. But I also know that my father's words are not the truth.

JOURNAL ENTRY 12

As a child, I was entranced by British ethologist Jane Goodall and imagined myself in Tanzania, sitting cross-legged for hours on end documenting the behavior of chimpanzees in the wild.

Later, during my first attempt to get a college degree, I declared myself an anthropology major and immersed myself in reading about primitive cultures.

So when my friend Lisa Thurston told me about Patricia Symonds, I was immediately drawn to her story. But I have to admit I was also shocked to discover that she'd become a Brown professor at age sixty. Ten years ago, at the comparatively youthful age of thirty-nine, I abandoned the idea of pursuing a doctorate because I doubted that any university would hire someone as old as me.

"OUR DOUBTS ARE TRAITORS, AND MAKE
US LOSE THE GOOD WE OFT MIGHT WIN,
BY FEARING TO ATTEMPT."

—William Shakespeare

PATRICIA SYMONDS
ANTHROPOLOGIST

Convinced by teachers that she wasn't smart, Patricia Symonds left school at age seventeen. Twenty-five years later, she finally resumed her education. Translating a lifelong interest in people into a career as an anthropologist, she spent eighteen months in her mid-fifties living in a bamboo house and doing fieldwork in northern Thailand. She's been teaching at Brown University for more than a decade.

Refreshingly unpretentious, she's wearing a T-shirt, a pair of old plaid shorts and not a speck of make-up. She looks like what she is—someone as comfortable in the mountains of Southeast Asia as in an Ivy League classroom.

The nuns in school used to tell me I was stupid. I believed them. Sometimes I still think to myself, "I have a Ph.D. and I've pulled the wool over someone's eyes."

I was born in the port city of Liverpool, England, and grew up during World War II. I'm not good with dates, but I was seven or so when it began. Dad was in the Navy. He was always at sea, never at home.

Every night, we had to go down into an Anderson shelter to sleep, which made me very claustrophobic. (During the war, government-issued Anderson shelters were distributed to people living in areas expected to be bombed by the Germans. They were constructed from curved metal sheets and half-buried in the ground.) I was scared. We all had torches—what Americans call flashlights—and I would take my torch under my covers and read. Since I was little, I have read voraciously. I'm miserable without books. I think reading was one of those things, in a way, that helped me survive. I would get into books like *Little Women* and imagine I was somewhere else.

One night our whole street was bombed. We had to get out of the shelter and be evacuated. We couldn't go down our pathway because of the incendiary bombs, so we had to go over a fence to get to a local church. I remember walking down the street with my mother, pushing my brother and sister in a pram. When we got to the church, my sister and I went in, but they wouldn't let my brother inside because he had the measles. My mother took him to the hospital; he had nowhere else to go. I was very upset. Maybe because of the war and all the bombing, I've always been interested in people and in why people kill things. I don't even like to kill an ant.

During the day, we still went to school. I remember once when I was nine or ten being taken to the Liverpool Museum on a school trip. I loved the museum. There was an old carousel horse inside that you could get on and ride. This might sound crazy, but I would get on that horse and think about where I wanted to go. I would go traveling! (She laughs.) This particular day I didn't want to leave, and I ended up getting locked inside. I don't know how I got out, but someone must have found me.

Then when I was eleven, I took a "scholarship"—a test to see if one is smart enough to go to a special school. At a scholarship school, you get a certificate at seventeen and then go onto university. If you didn't get a scholarship, at fourteen you left school and got a job.

When I took the scholarship, I passed. I was sent to a school called Broughton Hall. We had to wear a uniform, a navy blue pleated gym slip with a light blue blouse. My family could only afford one, so every night my mother would scrub the spots off and I would wear it again the next day.

In the beginning, I was doing okay. I think I was fifth in my class. But then things got bad at home. My mother and father fought; you couldn't keep anything on the mantelpiece. They divorced when I was fifteen. By the time I left school, I was something like thirty-third in the class.

The school was good. The teachers were good. But I was very curious, always asking questions. When we learned about the crusaders, for instance, I remember asking, "Do you think God would want them to kill people?" The questions I asked were not the kinds of things the nuns wanted to hear!

We also had things like domestic science where they taught us to sew. I was hopeless. I would sew something and then have to take the stitches out. I wasn't good at math either.

Once, though, we had a bishop come to the school. We were told we had to be very good, very respectful. I asked him about God being up there and all that sort of stuff. Two minutes after the bishop left, I was outside the door again for something I had done or said. Then the vice-headmistress came by and asked, "What are you doing? I was just coming 'round to congratulate you. The bishop said you were a very intelligent young woman asking very intelligent questions." That made me think maybe I wasn't as stupid as the nuns said.

Another thing that happened was that I took a three-hour geography exam. Geography was my favorite subject. It wasn't just about maps; it was about Africa and other cultures. I answered all the questions and got the highest score in the class. But then the nuns accused me of cheating. They didn't think I was smart enough to get the highest grade.

At seventeen when I was supposed to take our school certificate exam, the nuns wouldn't let me take the test. I think they thought I would disgrace the school. I never could have gone to university anyway. No one in my family had ever gone; I didn't know anyone who had.

Instead, because I liked kids, the nuns told me to be a nanny; but to be a nanny, you had to go through two years of training. Two years! They sent me to the Mabel Fletcher Technical School. Classes were three days a week. The rest of the time we taught in a nursery school, which I loved.

After I finished technical school, I had to take the National Nursery Certificate. Something happened, though. Maybe one of the students had gotten injured. I can't remember. We were all terrible wrecks when we went to take it. I did not pass. Many of us didn't. I decided not to re-take the exam; I was sure I would fail again. But the teachers made me, and I did fine. After getting my certificate, I got a job in a nursery.

Around this time, I met my first husband in a library in Liverpool. He was an American with the Air Force, and I was a G.I. bride. We got married in a Catholic Church and went to live in Leigh, not too far from Liverpool. It was the first time I'd ever lived away from home. I was twenty at the time.

Less than a year later, when my daughter Susan was still a baby, we came on a ship to America. We moved to Providence, where my husband's family was. In England everyone lives in little brick houses. In Providence, we lived in a three-tenement house. I'd never seen such a thing.

When Susan was eight and my second daughter, Karen, was four, we moved to Winston-Salem, North Carolina, where my husband had been accepted to medical college. People were always asking me where I'd gone to school and I'd say, "Oh, yes, I went to the Mabel Fletcher School in England." I didn't tell them I was a nanny.

I had to work, so I got a job in an obstetrics clinic. I was so bored. People would come in and I'd write down their names, how many weeks pregnant they were, and all this other stuff. Then one day the doctor called me into his office. I thought, "Oh my God, what have I done?" You know, like the nuns calling me out into the hall.

But then he said, "You're too intelligent to stay in this job. I think we should help you get another one, get a little bit more training so you'll be able to do something else." I thought, "Is this man crazy? What's going on here?" When he asked what level I'd gone through in school, I lied. I said I'd had two years of college. He said, "Okay then. Can you look into a microscope?" I told him I could try.

So I did a two-year training program in cytotechnology, learning to read slides. I passed and got a job at Wake Forest University Hospital. Eventually the people who trained me left, and I trained other people. I liked the job very much. We had a nice lab, a nice community. But I was always scared. I didn't think I was an intelligent woman. I could read these slides and could teach other kids to do it, but I thought I just had a skill. That's all. I still had never really got my confidence.

I worked at the hospital three and a half years until my husband graduated. Then we went back to Providence for his residency in ophthalmology. I was pregnant with my youngest daughter, Deborah, but still had to work. You know how it is. I found a job right away at Rhode Island Hospital and worked there until the day I delivered.

When my husband finished his residency, I left him. I'd had enough. It wasn't quite that simple, but I think I just felt that I had put my life on hold for fifteen years and didn't want to do it anymore. By this time, Susan was fifteen, Karen was ten and Deborah was four.

Then I met Alan. His wife had breast cancer, and I watched him take care of her. He was wonderful. So good. It was very, very touching. After she died, we eventually got married.

A short while later, Alan took me on a business trip to Mexico City. I was in my mid-thirties and had hardly traveled at all. Along with some other wives, I went to the National Museum of Anthropology. The museum was amazing. Pre-Columbian—stuff like that. When you went upstairs, there were all these wonderful full-sized dioramas of tribal homes. I met a couple there from Rhode Island—a lawyer and his wife. As I was looking at one of these exhibits, I said to both of them, "I am so overwhelmed. I want to learn and learn all about this."

The lawyer turned to me and said, "Well, why don't you?"

"You know what?" I replied. "That's exactly what I'm going to do."

When I came home, I told Alan. He encouraged me to go back to school, but I told him I couldn't. When he asked why not, I said, "Because I've got no high school, and I would never be able to pass any exams. I've been able to fake my way through up until now, but I won't be able to fake this."

"Do me a favor," he said. "Just go."

The University of Rhode Island had a continuing education program right in the middle of Providence. I waited months before doing anything. Finally, I went down and talked to a woman there. She was sitting behind a big desk, and I remember my feet tapping nervously on the rug as we spoke. I told her I wanted to go back to school. She asked me where I'd studied before. "In England," I said.

"Have you had any college?" she asked. When I told her I hadn't, she said, "Well, all you have to do is make out an application and give us a copy of your high school certificate."

I was sitting there in her office—I'll never forget it—and I said to her, "I have no high school certificate." I didn't cry, but I was very close to tears.

"Oh well," she said matter-of-factly. "Then you'll just have to take a GED."

After she finished explaining to me what a General Equivalency Diploma was, I said to her that I didn't think I could pass. She looked at me like I was crazy. Then she told me where to go, who to see, and gave me a letter to give to the person.

So I took her letter, signed and sealed in an envelope, and off I went with it that same day. I moseyed over to a brick church. It was not in a poverty-stricken area, but it was not in a great area either. Blue-collar, I think you'd call it.

The woman I'd been told about was there. In her office was a table rather than a desk, and she was sitting sort of sideways to it. It's funny to remember all these things. She had it set up so that her door was always open and she could see what was going on in the main room, where most of the people were working one-on-one. I went in and gave her the letter. She said to me, "I'd like to try something. Next week, I want you to take the exams one at a time so we can tell where you're at and what we need to do." Then she told me to go out and mingle with the people in the main room. Before I knew it, I was coaching this Italian guy.

The next week I went and took the tests for English, social studies and history. The last one was math. Alan and I were up half the night before going over algebra and mathematics. He's a brilliant guy, very good at math. But I didn't know anything. I couldn't even figure out what a percentage was. It was terrible. Anyway, I went back the following day and struggled through the math part.

After I finished the test, the woman told me to come again on Monday to find out what I should do next. But when I returned after the weekend and walked into her office, she said, "Congratulations! You're in the ninetieth percentile in everything except math."

"I knew it," I said. "I told you I couldn't do math."

"But you have done it," she said. "You've passed!"

I didn't quite understand.

"You read extremely well," she said. "And if you can read and I give you an article to answer questions on, you can answer those questions." I'd done that on the English and the social studies tests. I knew very little about American history, for example, but the questions they asked were on the articles they gave you. You didn't have to know everything.

Then the woman handed me my GED. I still have the certificate. I couldn't believe it; I was so excited. But once again I thought I'd pulled the wool over someone's eyes.

Afterward, I went back to see the person at the University of Rhode Island and showed her my certificate. She smiled at me as if to say, "I knew you were going to do that." My plan was to start classes there the following September.

Not too long after this, though, I went to dinner with some friends at a restaurant. One of them turned to the waiter, who was an older gentleman, and said, "Don't you go to Brown University?"

He said, "Yeah. I'm working here to pay my way through school."

Surprised, I asked him, "How can you go to Brown when you're older?"

"Oh, it's a great thing," he said. "It's called the Resumed Undergraduate Education Program."

I said, "Oh well. I couldn't go there. I haven't had any undergraduate education to resume!"

He told me I should apply anyway; and I thought to myself, "I wonder what would happen if I did?"

Eventually, I applied. I didn't think I'd get in. I didn't have any grades from anywhere. I got a recommendation from the doctor I had worked for at Rhode Island Hospital, and I got another one from this person whose course I had audited at the Rhode Island School of Design. But besides this, all I had was the GED.

Then I got called for an interview. It was a hot May day and I had on a pink suit. The school was only seven blocks from my house, but I drove. I couldn't find a parking space, and it was coming time for my appointment, so I was a wreck. Finally I drove back home, parked in the driveway and ran the seven blocks to Brown. The interview went well. But because I couldn't imagine I'd get in, I didn't think any more about it.

Then one day in the middle of the summer I got this letter saying I'd been accepted. Alan was out racing in his boat. When he came in, he looked at me and asked if I was okay. "I've been accepted to Brown!" I screamed. It was just so exciting.

I started at Brown in 1975. When I went to the campus in September, I kept thinking, "This is amazing. This is such a lovely, benevolent place."

At first I thought I would just take two classes. I took a freshman writing class and an anthropology course. Even though I didn't really know what anthropology was, I knew it had to do with people.

The writing class you could take at your own speed, and halfway through the semester, I was done. The woman gave me an A. She said, "You didn't really need this English course." Truthfully, to this day, I still think I need help with English.

In the anthropology class, everything was going great. Then we had the midterm. I froze. I don't remember anything until the professor said, "Hand in your papers." I hadn't even answered the questions!

I went to the teacher afterward and told him what had happened on the test. He said, "Oh, I thought you were doing very well in the class. Just keep on going." I got a B in that course, which was great.

After the first semester, I thought, "Hey, if this is what it's like, I can take four classes next time." I didn't want to be doing this until I was a hundred. So the following semester that's what I did.

Four years later, in 1979, at the age of forty-seven, I graduated magna cum laude.

My plan was to go right onto graduate school to get my master's and Ph.D. in anthropology. I got into Boston University and started there in October. Alan rented me an apartment in Boston, but he and the kids stayed behind in Providence.

Then Alan came up and told me he wanted a separation. He'd had enough. Part of it, I think, was that we had seven kids between us and Alan had been taking on most of that while I was in school.

I was devastated. I couldn't eat. As the days went by, I got thinner and thinner. I got through that semester at BU, but I don't know how. At the beginning of November, I told Alan that I was going to finish the semester and then I was going to quit school. I couldn't go on. He could see how I was. Everyone could.

Alan came for Christmas. We've always had Christmas Eve together with the kids, and we had a lovely dinner. He was going to leave for the motel, but I said, "Why don't you just stay?" He didn't stay that night, but he invited me to spend New Year's Eve with him. I was thin as a rail and got some very nice clothes. I dressed to a T. I did my eyes and everything. We went to a concert and then a restaurant on Newbury Street in Boston. Soon after this, we got back together.

From 1980 to 1982 I stayed home to take care of the kids. But by this time, even the younger ones were in school. I didn't have any intellectual stimulation and needed it desperately.

Finally, in '82, I asked Alan how he would feel about my going back to get a Ph.D. I told him I would try and get into Brown rather than going off to Boston again. He agreed. I applied and got in pretty quickly, but I was scared. I didn't want to lose him again.

After finishing my coursework for my master's degree, I had to do some fieldwork and write a thesis. Because of Alan, I wanted to stay in Providence. I had worked at an obstetrics clinic there—the Allen Berry Health Care Center—where several of the patients were Hmong refugees from Thailand. That's how I got interested in the Hmong. Many of the women had never been looked at by a man before, not even by their husbands. I decided to write my thesis on Hmong birth.

I spent the summer of '84 interviewing pregnant Hmong women. One day I went into a young woman's home who was just fifteen years old. She was sitting on a chair with her legs apart. I wanted to interview her husband as well, but he wasn't home. Only her mother-in-law was there. I asked when her baby was due. I didn't speak any Hmong then, but I'd become friendly with a woman named Iab who translated for me. I'm still friends with her to this day. Anyway, the girl said she was waiting for her cousin to take her to the hospital. She was almost ready to pop! I said, "Oh my goodness. I have my car outside. Why don't I take you?"

So we got in my car and went to the hospital. When we arrived, she had to go upstairs right away. I asked the girl's permission to come. She said that I could. Then there was this discussion with the mother-in-law, who also said that I could go with them. We all had to put on gowns and masks because the girl had had hepatitis and there was some worry about the baby. After she got to the birthing room, the doctor said, "She's just about ready, but it's time for my lunch. I'm going to do an episiotomy."

Iab was translating, and the mother-in-law said, "No. No episiotomy." The girl never made one peep. Not one peep. I thought this was weird. Then she moaned a little bit, and the mother-in-law went over and said something to her.

I asked Iab what was happening, and she said, "Oh, the mother-in-law just told her she can't make any noise because the spirits will hear and the baby won't come out."

The doctor said, "If she hasn't delivered by one o'clock, I'm going to do an episiotomy anyway." As he said that, fortunately, the baby came out.

It was all very interesting to me. The mother-in-law was there. Not the girl's mother. Not the father. The girl wasn't allowed to make a sound. I said to myself, "This is what I want to go out and look at for my Ph.D."

Once I finished my master's thesis and the coursework for my Ph.D., I had to do the fieldwork for my dissertation. I was fifty-four at this point. I'd applied for and gotten some funding, and my plan was to go to Thailand.

Alan had been diagnosed with a medical condition and was upset I was going. But I'd talked to his doctor, who assured me that he was going to be fine, and I'd already made the plans. This was in October of '86.

I'd never done something like this before. I had a camera, some clothes and a destination. That's about it. I had written my undergraduate honors thesis on the Queen Charlotte Islands and had spent the summer of '78 there. But this was much different. I was petrified.

Alan arranged everything. I went first class from California to Thailand. I was on United Airlines, and they took care of me like you wouldn't believe. Alan had also gotten me a reservation at a hotel in Bangkok—the Oriental. It's the fanciest hotel you could ever wish to be in.

When I got off the plane, the Oriental had a limo waiting to drive me to the hotel. It was after midnight. On the ride from the airport to downtown Bangkok, I could see all these people on the street eating and naked kids dancing. The smells coming from the klongs—canals where people live in stick houses—were terrible. I thought, "What am I doing here?"

But when I got to the hotel, two men brought fruit to the room and a silk robe was on the bed. The breakfast just appeared in my room in the morning. It was wonderful. I ate all my meals in the hotel and didn't go out much. I stayed at the Oriental for a week. God knows what it cost.

I knew a doctor who worked with the Hmong, and he had a research associate named Usanee. Usanee called me up one day and said, "My friend Pao and I would like to take you out so you can see a little bit of the area."

They took me to a crocodile farm and to see the elephants. You know, tourist places. We had a really great time and became fast friends. When I go back, I always stay at Pao's house.

We also visited the Chao Phraya River. There were barges and people and dogs floating in it. Just an incredible sight. Then I went up with them to Chiang Mai, a Thai town in the valley, and to the Tribal Research Council, where I was supposed to get permission to do my fieldwork. At the time I was planning on staying for a year. This was just the first week.

But then one of my daughters called and said, "Mom, Alan's not happy at all." As I said, he'd been having medical problems and was upset that I'd left. I stayed at the Oriental that night and flew home the next day.

Alan was really grateful that I'd come back. I said to him, "Look, I'm going to go again another time, but I wanted to make sure you were okay."

The October '86 trip was really good. It made me familiar with Thailand and made it much easier when I returned. But it was a false start.

In January of '87, I went to Thailand again. This time I didn't stay at the Oriental. A friend of mine, Nina, was back there doing a post-doctorate thing. She told me where to stay and helped me find a guesthouse in Chiang Mai. It was clean and cheap. She also introduced me to many scholars and some of her informants in a different tribe who knew a lot of Hmong. But after three months I still hadn't found the right place to settle down and begin my fieldwork.

Then, in March, Alan decided to visit for my birthday. He came with me as I looked around. One day we went with Nina and one of her informants, Asue, who has since become a dear friend, to this place that I call Flower Village, a Hmong village in northern Thailand.

The Hmong live high up in the hills. It's quite a trip to get up there, more than two hours by truck. This was during the dry season. We all went up to Flower Village to have a look. There was a funeral going on, but they let us come in. They were very nice. Alan said, "I like this place." But Nina was worried that the village was high up in the mountains and that I wouldn't be able to get out during the rainy season. She thought I'd go crazy.

Alan went home, and despite Nina's concerns, I went back to Flower Village to ask if it would be okay if I stayed there. First I went to the Hmong themselves. They said, "Oh yeah, you can come." Then I had to get permission from the county and the town. Everyone said it was okay.

I couldn't communicate much at first. The summer before, I had gone to the University of Michigan and studied Hmong all day every day. But getting the tone right was so hard. I would think I was asking for a drink of water and I would be asking for a drink of dog! To me it sounded like the same thing. At first the people in the village would laugh at me. But the wife of the chief had a younger cousin, Mai, who sat with me and signed and helped me learn.

As time went on, they all helped me and corrected me if I said something wrong. Then they even started struggling to learn my language. I could interact with them, but I could never learn everything. Their ideas are very different; their culture is very different.

I lived with the chief's family in a bamboo house. They wouldn't let me live by myself. Because it was the chief's house, part of it was built up on stilts, and that's the part where I stayed. I slept on the floor in a sleeping bag.

Every single morning I took notes as I sat on the porch and had my tea. The oldest daughter got up early each day to make rice, and she would make sure there was boiling water for me. They all knew, they all respected what I was doing there.

I would also write a letter home to Alan every morning. I saved all these. He wrote me every day as well. I would pick up his letters and mail mine when I went down into the valley. Once a month, even in the wet weather, the villagers would put chains on their trucks and take me down the mountain.

Alan came two or three times. It was hard to stay in the village. No lights. No electricity. No running water. We got up at sunrise and went to bed at sundown.

I was there a year and a half. When I first went, people weren't very open to me. But when I left in '88, all the women stood by the truck and cried.

After I got back to Providence, my mentor retired. Brown needed someone to teach his Southeast Asian course and hired me in 1992. I was sixty years old. The course turned out to be very successful and has gone on semester after semester.

I also teach an anthropology course on HIV and AIDS. The disease is very bad in Thailand. There are at least a million people with it, many of them Hmong. I taught this class with another mentor of mine until she retired three years ago. Now I teach it by myself.

When I first started teaching, I was so frightened. In the Southeast Asian course, there were some students who had spent a lot of time in that part of the world. The very first day I said something about Buddhism and made a mistake. Someone said, "Professor Symonds, you're wrong." I thought, "Oh my God, these kids are smarter than I am"—that whole thing of feeling stupid again. But then I thought about it a minute and I said to the kids, "That's really good. I like it when you let me know I'm making a mistake." They were great. It was a great class. I've been teaching at Brown now for more than ten years.

I've also been back to Thailand many, many times. When I first went there, I was afraid to leave the Oriental Hotel. Now I have a mother and a father in Flower Village. They're my family; they accept me as I am.

You know that geography exam the nuns said I cheated on? And the night I got locked inside the Liverpool Museum? And the tribal exhibits I was so excited by in Mexico City? Well, what I'm doing now is like an extension of those things. But years ago, when I first went to see about getting into the University of Rhode Island, I never dreamed I could do all this. Never. ✑

BESIDES TEACHING AT BROWN, Patricia has also authored numerous articles on the Hmong, HIV/AIDS and the anthropology of gender. She is currently publishing a book based on her dissertation. In 1998 she was diagnosed with breast cancer, but, after chemotherapy and a lumpectomy, she is now free of the disease. In 2000 she taught on a Semester at Sea voyage. Her most recent e-mail communication to me was posted from an internet café in Laos.   [P.B.]

JOURNAL ENTRY 13

I've been working on the introduction to my book. I want my sentences to pierce people's hearts, to set free the wild cuckoo bird trapped within. But instead of leaving lunatic feathers in their wake, my words fall flat and land with a thud upon the page. How I wish I could write like Gabriel García Márquez. Only he could use a phrase like "lunatic feathers" and make it sound like pure music.

JOURNAL ENTRY 14

I recently read that Native-American author Beth Brant was driving somewhere before her fortieth birthday when a bald eagle flew in front of her car and told her she was supposed to be a writer. She changed the direction of her life and stepped back on the gas. For most of us the signposts are much more subtle. More often than not, I suspect, one misses them altogether.

That said, several of the women I've interviewed—Linda Bach, Jean Kelley, Jo Fuchs Luscombe and Patricia Symonds—were similarly approached by a casual acquaintance who innocently uttered a few words and altered the trajectory of their lives.

Here's what I wonder. Were these four women—five, including Beth Brant—approached at the precise moment they were prepared to take their respective leaps? If they had heard these words of encouragement a month earlier, would they have been able to respond? Or would the words have been dismissed as pure folly? In my case, I think it's very possible that I wouldn't be writing this particular book if I had read about Wini Yunker even one day before I did.

JOURNAL ENTRY 15

One afternoon I opened my mailbox and found a clipping from the Ladies Home Journal inside. A friend who knew I was writing about late bloomers not only took the trouble of cutting it out for me but also made the effort to deliver it to my house. The article was about a woman named Evelyn Gregory who became a flight attendant at the age of seventy-one.

Right away, I sat down and wrote Evelyn a letter introducing myself and asking whether she'd be interested in sharing her story for my book. When I didn't hear back from her, I waited two more years before daring to try again. (Isn't that silly?) When I finally got the courage to call her, we immediately clicked. I was floored when she said she remembered who I was and was eager for me to interview her. I caught up with her at a Philadelphia hotel.

"DARE AND THE WORLD ALWAYS YIELDS; OR
IF IT BEATS YOU SOMETIMES, DARE IT AGAIN,
AND IT WILL SUCCUMB."

—William M. Thackery

EVELYN GREGORY
FLIGHT ATTENDANT

After the death of her husband of forty-two years, a successful career in banking and a brief hiatus as a self-proclaimed
beach bum, Evelyn Gregory fulfilled her childhood dream
and became a flight attendant. Initially rejected by several
carriers, she was hired by Mesa Airlines in 1999 and earned
her wings at the age of seventy-one. Today, she divides her
time between teaching other flight attendants and making
regular flights on US Airways Express out of Charlotte,
North Carolina.

Affectionately known as "Nana," she's the grandmother of
seven and looking forward to becoming a great-grandmother
in the fall. Everywhere she goes, she inspires others.

I always had this longing to be a flight attendant. I just thought it
was so romantic. Back when I was in high school, a group of us
would get together and ride by the airport six or seven miles outside of Durham, North Carolina. It used to be total entertainment
—to watch the planes land. Even in my younger days, I always
wanted to travel.

So I just grew up thinking that this is what I wanted to do. But
I remember talking to my dad about it, and he said flying was dan-
gerous. Deep down, I think he felt that nice girls didn't do this. He
never did say that, but I think that is what he thought. Also, back
then to be a flight attendant, you had to be a registered nurse. And

my dad said to me, "You know, if you go get your degree in nurs-ing and aren't hired by the airlines, you'll end up as a nurse, and that's the hardest job ever." So I didn't pursue it at all. It went clear out of my mind until my husband died. The thing that's interest-ing is that my brother Harold now has his own plane. I was also talking to my sister Carolyn a few years ago, and she said, "You know, I always wanted to be a flight attendant, too." So I guess that love of flying came through to all of us.

After I graduated from high school, my business teacher got me a job out at Duke University. I was secretary to twelve Divinity professors. What is really neat is that I got to go to Duke that year. I worked part-time and went to school part-time. For a nominal fee, I took classes from May of '45 until the next year.

I'd actually been accepted to East Carolina University before I graduated from high school, but that was a long way off—all the way to the other end of the state. (She laughs.) I didn't end up going. I didn't think that my dad wanted me to go. He never said I shouldn't. He didn't discourage me. He just didn't encourage me.

My dad came of age during the Depression, and truly my whole concept of work comes from him. He's the one who said to me, "Always be there. If the company you work for didn't need you, you wouldn't have the job." And that has been my philosophy. It has been very unusual for me in all the years I've worked to take a day off.

After my year at Duke, I got married. I'd just turned nineteen. I knew of my husband, Coy, growing up; he lived around the corner from us. But he was three years older than I was, and I didn't meet him until after he got out of the Navy. He took part in D-Day—the invasion at Normandy—and he was just a brazen little old sailor. Cute as could be. We started dating, and that was it.

When we first got married, we lived out at the Gregory family farm. There was a big lake behind us, and we'd go down and fish and play in the boat. It was a lot of fun. I had a job at an insurance company. But after a few months, I heard that the old Fidelity Bank in Durham was looking for someone. That's when I got into banking. I was secretary to the president and ended up working at Fidelity almost ten years.

During that time, Coy and one of his brothers bought a single-engine plane. A Luscomb. I never flew with them, but I'd go to the airport and watch—there was still that little part inside of me that wanted to fly.

One of the first times I ever actually flew was in the late fifties. I went on an Eastern Air Lines flight from Durham to Indianapolis to see my husband's brother. I remember flying over a huge forest fire and seeing the red burning embers over such a wide area. After watching how the stewardess performed her duties, I became more fixed on my desire to become a flight attendant. Even then, however, I did not dwell on the idea. I thought I would have no chance since I was older and married. I was in my late twenties or early thirties at that point.

Because Coy and I were the only ones of the Gregory clan in Durham who didn't have children, when the family decided to buy a laundry and dry cleaning plant in Lincolnton, northwest of Charlotte, we were the ones who were voted on to run that. We went up there in '57.

After moving to Lincolnton, I didn't work. I'd never lived anywhere other than Durham, and I wanted to take a little time to get to know the place. I also wanted children so badly, but I'd been told I couldn't have them. So I was shocked and delighted the next year to learn I was pregnant. Kelly was born in April of '59, right before my thirty-second birthday. Right away, in October of '61, Ken came along. Then Jennie was born in July of '63. I had two in diapers at the same time. It was so exciting. The years when the children were little are a blur. I just remember it as wonderful times, fun times—the Christmases and all that kind of thing.

Then in 1971, my next-door neighbor, who was the senior vice-president of Carolina First National Bank in Lincolnton, told me he needed someone to help him in the trust department. I took the job. My youngest was only in second or third grade, but Coy was able to be there when the kids got home from school.

I'd only been working full-time for eight months or so when Coy had his first massive heart attack. He was forty-seven and I was forty-four. I felt it was a blessing that I was working. Coy got about during those first years, but he never was able to run his business after that. He couldn't lift heavy stuff. My son would have loved to have taken over, but he wasn't old enough, so the business closed. It was very traumatic for all of us.

After Coy had that first bad heart attack in '71, I just sat and bawled. I mean it really hurt. I no longer had a security blanket. I had a husband who was ill and I had three kids. So work was a necessity for me.

On the weekends I got a second job at one of the local motels. I'd go in bright and early in the morning and work until two or three o'clock at the front desk. I was also very active in the American Institute of Banking, which is how I got into the teaching that I enjoy so much now. I taught banking courses for three area colleges. I did that at night for many years. Even though I didn't have a college degree, I knew banking.

We were in Lincolnton until the kids were pretty much grown up. Then the bank transferred me to Denver, North Carolina, as a manager. We built a house on Lake Norman.

Coy was so sick. He helped me with the house plans, but he never even got to walk to our waterfront lot, which was right across the street. He died on Mother's Day in 1989, a year and a half after we moved there.

Again, my salvation was that I was working. When Coy died, I accepted it. He would not have wanted to remain in the condition he was in. I wanted to quit work and stay home, or get a leave, but he said, "No, you aren't going to do that." He didn't want me to baby him. I think he knew he was dying.

Afterward, my dear friends Patsy and George took me under their wing. They'd invite me over. Going home to an empty house was the worst time ever, and they knew that. What do you do when you get home? You get your clothes ready for the next day and go to bed. I can't say I was depressed, because I knew what had happened was best for Coy, but I was lonely. Two of my kids were nearby and my co-workers were wonderful. But it was still hard.

I worked three-and-half more years until I retired at the end of February '93. I was sixty-five. Counting the ten years in Durham, I worked in banking thirty-two-and-a-half years. The last six or so I was an assistant vice president and branch manager. I had the best situation. I was able to help some people get loans—maybe their car was a clunker and they needed a new one—and to help others invest.

At the time I retired, I thought, "Okay, this is going to be great." Patsy and George had a place at Myrtle Beach, which is about three-and-a-half to four hours from Denver. So I bought a vacation home there—a thirty-two-foot single-wide trailer—and became a beach bum. My idea of retirement was to hunt seashells, play golf, and do a lot of walking. That was basically it. I just thought it was going to be fun; and in the beginning, it was. One of my grand-daughters was recently talking about what a wonderful time they had that first year. They stayed the whole summer and were as brown as Indians.

The next year Patsy and George decided to build their own place and sold me their Park Model trailer, which was wider than the one I had. I could sit on my nice big screened-in porch, drink my coffee and smoke my cigarettes while I listened to the ocean. My mom, Ruth—a beautiful seamstress and a fine woman—was in a nursing home in Durham then. So I also went back and forth to look after her.

Then in 1995 my mom died at the age of ninety-three. Patsy and George were no longer living permanently at the beach. No one was there much. It was horrible. I was so lonely, I couldn't stand it. I waited a year and sold the place.

I came back to Denver and started volunteering at a nursing home. Deep down I felt a need to give something back because of how well my mom had been treated in Durham. I'd go polish patients' nails every other Tuesday. But the next week, more people would be gone; they'd be dead.

That's when I started thinking about being a flight attendant again. My good friends Peter and Terri worked for an airline and were always talking about flying. Peter was a pilot, and Terri was an international flight attendant. I told them how I'd always wanted to be a flight attendant, and they encouraged me. Peter was always saying, "Nana, you'd be the greatest."

So I applied. This was in October of '97. I'd just turned seventy. Terri and Peter told me to go online and see when there was going to be a recruiting session for US Airways. I did and signed up for one. The first interview was in a group. I must have done fine because from that group they chose some of the applicants to go to Pittsburgh for a second interview, and I was among those who were asked. In Pittsburgh, I had an individual interview. Afterward I was told I'd hear something in a few weeks.

I felt so confident. I thought no one could have more customer service experience than I did. Yes, I thought about my age. But having been involved in the hiring process at the bank, I knew you couldn't ask how old someone was. Of course, I had to put down when I graduated from high school, and they knew I didn't do that when I was three!

I was asked to come back for a third interview. But afterward I got a letter saying that even though my resume was impressive, they didn't have anything for me at that time. That's when I started applying everywhere—Comair, Piedmont, Delta, maybe even American. I don't remember exactly. I didn't get interviews with any of them. I got acknowledgements, but no encouragement. I was demoralized, but I wasn't going to give up. That was the thing. I knew I had what it took. I didn't cry or get upset; I was just determined.

Then I saw an ad in the Charlotte Observer for a gate agent with CCAir at Charlotte Douglas International Airport. I applied. When I first met the man who was hiring, I told him I wanted to be a flight attendant. He explained to me that they hired from within and that there was a probationary period of six months.

So I went through the probationary period as a gate agent. I enjoyed that, by the way. But I still wanted to fly. Then a week and a day before my six months were up, I learned that there was going to be another flight attendant class. Mesa Air Group had bought CCAir, and my supervisor said, "I understand Mesa is hiring." She suggested that I go talk to one of people there.

At that time, Mesa had a place up on Concourse A in Charlotte, a crew lounge where they could do interviews. So on my lunch hour I went up and talked to a young lady there. She handed me a paper and I filled it out. It was just a regular application form. Then I gave it back to her. She glanced at it and said, "When would you like to go to ground school?"

I said, "Just like that?" Those were my words. "Just like that?"

She said, "Yeah. I know all about you." My supervisor must have called her up beforehand.

I was so excited. I gave my gate agent supervisor two weeks' notice. I don't believe in just walking off the job. Then about three weeks later I went to ground school in Phoenix.

In Phoenix, Mesa had bought an older motel it used as a dormitory. The Del Rio. It was delightful. We had such a good time there. They had fruit trees—lemons and grapefruits and figs. At night after our class, all of us trainees would get together and cook. We had an outdoor gas grill in a grassy area with a canopy. There were pilots there as well. I remember one night one of the pilots cooked ribs and I made a chicken casserole and a fresh spinach salad. I also made homemade lemonade. They all thought it was the best thing.

Back then, ground school was three weeks. Everyone had to have a roommate. Until you graduate, you're always paired with someone else. Once you're out on your own, you get a single room. That's one of your perks. Anyway, my roommate was only eighteen years old. She turned nineteen while we were there. We had two twin beds. One day she met a boy at a grocery store in Phoenix and said to me, "Nana, he's invited me to a cookout tonight. What do you think?"

I said, "Well, I'm not your mom, and I'm not your grandmother. But I want his address and phone number just in case. Even though I don't have a car and can't get to you myself, I want to be able to dial 9 1 1." So she did. It was so cute.

I was determined to do well in ground school. I probably studied more than a lot of the other recruits. There's a tremendous amount of memory work, mainly city codes. They send you a big packet before you come. One code that was really funny was Newburgh, New York, which I'd never heard of before. It was SWF. I thought of it as "some weird folks." I didn't know anybody there, so for me they were weird. (She laughs.) Louisville, Kentucky, was SDF, which became "some dear friends" because I have friends there. That's the way I memorized them. I'd take a little recorder and I'd say, "SDF." Then I'd pause and say, "Louisville, Kentucky." Anywhere I was in the car, I played that tape. So I did just fine. I got my wings on May 24, 1999, at the age of seventy-one.

At first, I flew with someone else, so there was a lot of comfort there. It's called an IOE, an initial operating experience. It went great. I had a good person with me. Then on June 4th I had my solo debut. It was on a fifty-person jet. I'd been president of our American Institute of Banking chapter that included seven counties and had spoken before two hundred people or more. I had never been afraid to talk in front of people in my life. But that very first day when I went out by myself, I was a nervous wreck. My voice was quivering: "Good evening ladies and gentlemen." I was all choked up. But then I said, "Excuse me, I've just got to tell you that this is my very first day by myself and I am *soooo* nervous. Please be kind to me." The passengers broke into spontaneous applause.

After this, it was just old hat. At first I was based out of Birmingham, Alabama. Wonderful people. The airline puts you in a hotel to start, but then you have to find a place to live. You've got to have a crash pad wherever you're based. I told one of the gate agents, a gorgeous girl named Kim, that I needed to find somewhere to sleep. She offered me her son Parker's Nintendo room with a three-quarter bed. I was only at Kim's house for six weeks or so before I got reassigned to Charlotte, which was my first choice. Usually it takes three months or so before you get to the place you want to be.

Then I heard that Mesa needed instructors, so I did ground school in Phoenix part-time. Within six months, I got into that. They knew I'd taught college. A woman named Kenda trained me for ground school. She also trained me to do IOE's. She taught me everything I know—at least about flying.

Teaching and flying is the best of both worlds. It thrills me to death to make new recruits comfortable. We all had to start somewhere. And maybe there's a little trick of the trade I can give someone to make something a little easier. I encourage new recruits to be patient, to give it a year.

I also get to be helpful with my passengers. My first concern is their safety. I'm sort of adamant about that. If I see them doing something that isn't safe, I say so. I literally screamed at a man one day. We were in the last few minutes of our flight and getting ready to land when he popped up like a jack-in-the-box. I said, "Sir. Sit!" I wasn't going to get out of my jump seat and break my neck. Oh me.

I'm still with Mesa. My ID is with Mesa, and they pay me. But Mesa has a code-share agreement to do these small commuter flights. So I fly with US Airways Express out of Charlotte. Sometimes I get physically tired, but not often. I don't think I get any more tired than people half my age. The only thing is that my feet hurt. It's like walking on concrete all day. But, really, you couldn't ask to be treated any better. They treat me like a dear grandmother.

I love my crews. They give me hugs. We work as a team. From CEO Jonathan Ornstein on down, the entire Mesa family has been so supportive.

I also love getting into this or that town and seeing new things. I remember how much fun some of us had in Washington. We hopped on the Metro and went to the Mall area and spent several hours at the Smithsonian and in the Air and Space Museum. Then we walked to Georgetown and had dinner at a little restaurant. Just a great day.

My daughter Kelly is a teacher, and couple of years ago her school kids wrote letters to me. They were so adorable. One said, "Did you crash yet?" Another said, "Did you see the desert?" Someone else asked, "How much gas does it take to fly?" These were second and third graders. I wrote them back individually in a letter—just a sentence each—but addressing them by name. Later, still in uniform, I went straight to Kelly's class and got to meet the kids. It was so cute. You could tell exactly who had asked which question.

Today on my flight from Detroit I was asked by a woman how long I'd been flying. I told her how fortunate I was that Mesa was willing to hire me at seventy-one and that I'll be starting my fifth year this coming May. She said, "Maybe this is something I can do when I retire." She's a registered nurse. It excites me to see someone get interested in the profession after watching me on duty. I even had a college president on one of my flights express a desire to do this when she retired. I always encourage people to pursue their dreams, no matter what their age. Just this year I was a guest on one of the demo flights for the new 700s. We went up to the Grand Canyon and did figure eights. It was awesome! ✍

JOURNAL ENTRY 16

Mom and I have been joking lately that life begins at eighty. (She turned eighty in April of 2003.) But seriously, for some people it might.

JOURNAL ENTRY 17

Since I began writing this book two years ago, I've made several changes in my life:

1. I've become fiercely protective of my time. In September of 2001, the same month my youngest son went to college, I quit my teaching job to write full-time. It was one of the best—and scariest—things I've ever done. I've pared my life down to what's really important to me: family, friends and working on this book.

2. I'm trying not to listen to my doubts. Early on in this project, I made a pact with myself to turn a deaf ear to my inner demons. Even though my doubts still flood over me on a regular basis and spill into my journal entries, I don't converse with them.

3. I've surrounded myself with people who believe in me. At this point, I'm like a tender plant. I need to be nurtured, not stepped on.

4. I've resolved not to lose momentum. I don't always write. Sometimes I make phone calls or travel arrangements. But every day I put some energy toward the book.

5. I'm making a habit of confronting my fears. When I feel afraid, I dive in rather than walk away. In the past two years I've done karaoke (I love to sing, but never had the courage to do it in front of people), had a big New Year's Eve bash (entertaining used to make me break out in a cold sweat) and tried gorgonzola cheese (the smell alone is frightening!). What does eating cheese have to do with writing books? The more I practice facing my fears, the easier it gets.

JOURNAL ENTRY 18

I heard about Mary Orlando from her son Sean. He spoke of his mother with such admiration for her midlife achievement and with so much love that I just had to meet her.

At first Mary's tale appealed to me because it didn't involve going back to school. But I've come to see that her story has greater significance for my book.

Biologically, historically and mythically, women are deeply connected with motherhood and home. Many of us—even those with professional careers and no children—yearn to have strong, caring relationships and to create a physical space where those we love can find sanctuary. Mary tried to do this twice. First, she did it according to society's vision and her religious upbringing. Then she set about doing it on her own terms. She's succeeded beyond her wildest hopes.

GO CONFIDENTLY IN THE DIRECTION
OF YOUR DREAMS! LIVE THE LIFE YOU'VE
IMAGINED.   —Henry David Thoreau (paraphrase)

MARY ORLANDO
BED & BREAKFAST PROPRIETOR

Raised in a large family that worked and played together, Mary Orlando hoped to replicate this lifestyle when she got married. At first she succeeded. But when her husband of twenty-nine years suddenly left her, the dream unraveled. Alone and working three jobs to support herself, she began to consider buying the historic home she'd lived in as a child and refurbishing it as a bed-and-breakfast. At the age of sixty-two, she opened the Mary Stuart House in Goshen, Connecticut. In making her vision a reality, she has not only brought her family back together but created a place where other people with children and pets can come and relax.

Soft-spoken and self-effacing, she has short brown hair and a wide, kind face. An accomplished cook and relaxed hostess, she makes guests feel welcome as soon as they walk in the door.

I always felt this house was my home. It was built in 1798 and was an inn through the early 1900s. According to family legend, my mom stayed here as a young girl and told her parents she wanted to buy it someday. The three of them rode in a horse and carriage from Torrington, Connecticut, where they lived. It's only a ten-minute drive now, but back then it would have probably taken all day to get here. My family bought the property—forty-three acres in all—when I was nine. So I grew up in this house, raised as the oldest of six children.

Back then it was a working dairy farm. In the barn we had any-where from thirty to forty-five cows, and we sold the milk. It seemed like there was always work to be done. Besides milking, there was haying and caring for all the other animals. We also had large gardens where we planted vegetables such as cucumbers, corn and potatoes. We made strawberry jam and dill pickles and preserved all sorts of produce to carry us through the winter months. Each Saturday morning we'd eat homemade donuts, and then my father would organize a household clean-up with all of us. So there was a feeling of daily accomplishment, which I loved.

We also weren't scattered as much as families are today. Every night we ate together as a family, with a special meal on Sunday. After dinner, we'd sit in the dining room and do our homework. We didn't go to our separate rooms to study. On holidays and special occasions, my family would gather around the large dining room table my father had built from a door. Neighbors who didn't have a place to go would join us. During the Christmas season, we'd also invite carolers to come inside for hot chocolate. Many adults in this community have recounted their memories of these times to me.

Until I purchased the house in 1997, the last time I lived here full-time was in eighth grade. In ninth grade, I went to a private boarding school. Then, when I was seventeen, I met my husband at Dean College in Franklin, Massachusetts.

We dated about three years. He was kind and gentle, and he took me out to dinner and the movies and bowling. I think I was attracted to him because he paid attention to me. I liked that he liked me.

We were married in October of '57. I was the first in my family to marry, so it was a very exciting time for my parents and siblings. It seemed like the entire town was involved with the wedding prep-arations. Several of my mother's friends had bridal showers for me and housed my guests, and the food was catered by a group of church women in the community.

The reception was here at the house, and a large tent was set up in the backyard. By then my father was a state representative; and besides running the farm, he had a nursery and landscaping business across the street. Prior to that, he'd been a stockbroker. So he knew a lot of people. I felt like all of Goshen was at my wedding.

When I got married, I hoped to have a large family. I wanted to work and play together, to share like I did when I was growing up. My husband and I eventually settled in Huntington Station, Long Island, and had five children—three boys and two girls. The oldest is now forty-one; the youngest is twenty-nine.

My life was comfortable for many years. Our house on Long Island was the last one on a dead-end street, a three-bedroom colonial on an acre of land that backed up to twenty acres of woods. My father-in-law put a cable ride in our backyard, which sloped downward. The kids would take this cable ride down to a tree house, which my father-in-law built as well, and have picnics there. We also had an above-ground pool. I thought it was a great place for the kids to grow up.

During those years, we had lots of wonderful neighborhood friends and lots of block parties and gatherings. Several of us moved in at once, and our children were all around the same age. There were many families back then where the mothers were home. We were all in the same boat—a different situation than we have today.

I was a stay-at-home mom for almost twenty years. I was quite busy with the children and their activities and had a variety of different interests. I was a church youth group chaperone and the leader of a two-year-old play group. Later, I joined both a volley-ball and a tennis league and took guitar lessons.

I thought about getting an early childhood education degree, and for a while I even trained with a teacher at the Montessori nursery school my three older children attended. But when I told my husband that I was planning to take two classes at night while he was at home, he said I'd be abandoning the children. I was so upset. The first night I cried all the way to school. I did two semesters, but then got pregnant again and gave up on the idea.

Gradually, I began to feel more and more discouraged and unappreciated. My husband would come in the door after work and ask what I did all day. I knew what I did all day. I hardly ever sat down. But he didn't value what I was doing for the family.

For about ten years or so before he left the marriage, he'd been working a lot longer hours—seventy or eighty hours a week. He was an aerospace engineer and was working at Grumman Aircraft on the LEM, the lunar module. When he was home, it seemed like all he did was sleep and eat. There were times I'd say to him, "If all I'm going to get is a paycheck, just mail it to me." That's terrible to say. There's probably a better way to phrase it. But for so many years, that's how I felt.

I remember one time, when he was working on a big project, he drove our camper to Grumman and lived in it for two weeks. The children never even knew he was gone! For so many years he'd been coming home after they went to bed and going to work before they woke up that they didn't even miss him. That was his life. It didn't include us. I never expected to be doing that much on my own. I thought I would have a partner, another adult to deal with whatever came along.

As my husband worked more hours, I became more and more independent. In a way, I think it helped me to be able to handle the divorce when it came. If I'd been counting on him during those years and all of a sudden he said, "I'm leaving," what would I have done?

I tried to make my husband happy. I felt it was my job. For years before he left, he'd say, "I'm not comfortable here." So I'd rearrange the room. I'd re-paint. I'd make special meals. I'd dress differently. I did everything I could think of to do. But after a while, nothing made a difference. I realize now that it had nothing to do with me or the house; he was just going in a different direction. I knew our marriage wasn't great; but I just thought, "Well, all couples have ups and downs and difficult times."

For our twenty-fifth wedding anniversary, our children surprised us with a dinner and invited our neighbors and friends. It was a wonderful evening and memorable for all their combined efforts. As I said, our marriage wasn't ideal; but I thought at this point we'd made it through.

Then, just a year or two shy of our thirtieth anniversary, my husband came to me and said he wanted a divorce. I remember I was standing in the front hallway. He told me he just didn't want to be married anymore.

I couldn't believe it. I was in shock. I knew he wasn't happy, but I had no idea he would go that far. I wondered what I had done wrong. I was still thinking it was my responsibility to make the marriage work. I felt so rejected. I couldn't understand how it got to that point. It didn't seem like it was that bad.

I didn't say much to anyone. People I saw every day didn't even know I was going through a divorce. I had a hard time adjusting to the fact that I had made a commitment and had failed in honoring it. I couldn't eat. I couldn't sleep.

Shortly after my husband left, my children planned a birthday party for me. I was still so devastated by this trauma that I couldn't celebrate. I didn't feel like I deserved a party. I felt so inadequate, so unloved. At the time I just couldn't believe that anyone—even my children—really cared.

For the first year I kept thinking my husband would change his mind, that he would come back. I kept dreaming that it was going to work out, that he would be happy with the family again. I was working part-time at the church as a secretary and finally went to talk to my pastor. I told him I was having trouble taking off my wedding band. He helped me make that break.

Over the next few years, my three older children married and moved to their own homes, and my youngest son, Sean, traveled to Europe. Then, when my youngest daughter was a senior in high school, she decided to move in with a girlfriend. There was nothing I could do. My husband supported her. I was very upset, very hurt. I wanted her to be happy, but I was upset that she was living with this particular family. I knew it was a questionable situation, and I was concerned for her welfare. Fortunately, my daughter was only with this girl for the summer. That was probably the hardest time for me, the lowest point.

Looking back, I realize that things were happening to me. I was not making my own decisions, not leading the way. I didn't have the self-esteem or the confidence.

Following the divorce, it was difficult financially. I had to borrow money from my family, use the savings I had started for my children and let my life insurance lapse. I also had to sell some jewelry and other valuables.

I continued to work as a church secretary and also did some medical transcription at home. But then I needed to bring in more income, so I got a third job at Brunswick Hospital in Amityville, about half an hour from where I lived. I did these three jobs for a couple of years before I started doing medical transcription full-time at St. Francis Heart Center in Roslyn, New York.

I was just walking along, trying to take care of the bills. It started to feel like I was on a hamster wheel. Gradually I began to realize that I was just working to pay expenses—and not living. I started asking myself how was I going to get away from that— have less expenses and more time for life. This was just building up over a few years of working many, many hours and not doing much beyond that.

During this same time, a year or so after the divorce, my mother got sick. She had emphysema. For five or six years, my siblings and I all took turns coming up here on weekends and taking care of her. My mom died in 1994.

After my mom passed away, my son Sean said, "Don't let anything happen to the house." That sort of stuck with me, but I didn't think buying it was something I could do.

My siblings and I put the house on the market. It was not in good shape. It needed a new heating system, new roof, new electrical wiring, new floors. That made it hard to sell. We also didn't want someone buying the property and tearing down the house. It was on the market two years, going more and more into disrepair.

Those two years I didn't come back here much. The family didn't get together much either. So the house not selling coincided with my realizing I wasn't doing anything with my life except paying the bills. I didn't have time to be with family and friends.

I guess in some way I was also becoming more of an individual, more sure of myself. As I said, I was starting to make choices for myself. I was planning on moving from Long Island anyway—just to shed the weight of it—when all of a sudden I thought this must be a message. I started thinking that maybe I could buy the house after all.

You could say I went back to Sean's vision. I felt that the house meant so much to him. But there were other little things that were also part of my decision. My oldest son, Gary, had been trying to find a bed-and-breakfast for his family to stay at, but all the ones he looked at didn't allow children. That didn't seem right to me—to have trouble finding a place to take your family for a vacation. I thought it would be nice to have someplace where travelers could come that would be like a home away from home, not like a hotel.

Then I talked to my brother-in-law. He said there was a lot of value in the house—that it was structurally sound. It didn't bother me that the house needed so much work. My grandfather had also set up a trust fund that my siblings and I inherited after my mom died. It had been growing all those years, and the market was doing well at that point. Perfect timing. I decided to sell some stock and put that money toward the house.

At the same time I was trying to buy this house, I was also trying to sell my house on Long Island. After a year of the Long Island house being on the market and not selling, my daughter Lesley and her husband decided to buy it. So Lesley bought her childhood home and went back there, and I bought my childhood home and came back here. That made it a lot easier. It really did.

I was sixty when I bought the house in 1997. Once I made the decision, there was a lot of support. Although some of my siblings weren't so positive, it wasn't as if they weren't supporting me. They just kept saying that it was a big project and a lot of work. I must have felt like I could do it, though. The more I overcame on my own, the more I felt what I'd chosen to do was possible. I always felt like there was a way. It's good to be realistic, but it's also good to be idealistic sometimes.

After buying the house, I continued to work on Long Island to support myself. I'd go down Tuesday night and work three thirteen-hour days, and then come back here Friday evening for a four-day weekend. Finally, in 1989 I got a job as a medical transcriptionist at Charlotte Hungerford Hospital, which is about a ten-minute drive from Goshen. I worked there two-and-a-half years while continuing the renovations.

As the vision of opening a bed-and-breakfast became stronger, the challenges became greater. It was a major job, and there were massive obstacles to surmount to bring the house up to code as a business. I had to deal with the Planning & Zoning Board, the Taxation Department, and the Health Department. Fire escapes were also an issue, as was getting the regulated size for the B&B sign near the road. The business end of it was probably the hardest thing for me.

I tried to do the most important projects first, the ones that would allow me to open and make the place livable. Most of all, I needed to do the plumbing, the heating, the roof and the kitchen.

The first electrician just gave up. The wiring in the house was so old. I had to find an electrician willing to handle a house with old wiring and bring it up to code.

I also had a carpenter come in for two weeks to start working on the kitchen. But when I returned from Long Island, he'd done so many things wrong that I had to let him go. He was cutting into support beams of the house. The ceiling wasn't aligned. Things like that. To get some of my down payment back, I had to go to court.

On Sean's advice, I hired a man named Bob Barwikowski, a wonderful builder who's very connected to the Goshen community. He's been with the renovation now for six years and went with me in front of all the town boards. I couldn't have done this without him. He and his family have become great friends of ours.

Besides Bob, there were the plumbers, the painter and the electrician—Ray and John, T.J. and Jimmy. The house renovation ideas just evolved. We all had so much fun together. We'd go from room to room deciding to do this and that. The men said they looked forward to coming to work here, that it didn't feel like work.

One weekend when I was on Long Island, T.J. painted the walls of the kitchen with a faux finish, changing them from a boring blue to a buttery yellow. It was his idea—a nice surprise for me when I returned. I loved it!

Then my family and friends came on board, along with many new friends. We had a great time. Sean was here a lot and sometimes brought friends from Brooklyn to help. One of his female painter friends cleaned up a wall mural that my mother had painted years before. She used a toothbrush to make sure it was done right without destroying it. My daughter Stephanie also came for a year from California.

All the rooms had to be redone. Each one had to be stripped of four or five layers of wallpaper and repainted. A wall unit in the living room had to be taken out before painting the walls, and the floor needed to be replaced as well before the wall unit was put back. We also put a bathroom in one of the second-floor bedrooms and built a new screened-in porch.

A multitude of women helped with the decorating. They're like family now—like a part of this house. I feel like it's their home, too. They'd go out and look for things at tag sales and flea markets. My friend Cyndi did all the window treatments. Another friend, Nancy, redecorated the great room as a rooster room. She bought a plate rack with rooster plates. My friends Linda and Andrea, as well as some of the guests, have given other roosters to me. There's a corner cabinet now filled with rooster items. Linda and Andrea and some of their other friends have also been working on the flower gardens.

This home has been a community effort. Lots of love, hard work and creative ideas have gone into it. We've had painting parties, deck building parties—all kinds of gatherings.

When we got near the end of the renovations and were ready to open the bed-and-breakfast, we had an open house here. We sent out a bulk mailing to the town so they could come see what we'd been doing with the house and all the changes that had been made. We also had local craftspeople come in and set up their tables, which is something I'd like to do more of as time goes on.

It was wonderful.

Two years ago, I had a family reunion here. About sixty family members and friends came from various parts of the country. My four sisters and their families all came. Only one niece and nephew couldn't make it. My brother and his wife were here, too. My son Kevin came from Florida with his wife and three girls. All my children were here. The kids were sleeping all over—in the main house, the little house out back, and the barn. The dairy barn now has two apartments, and we're renovating another section of it as a game room for use by the guests. No more cows.

My one sister who's a photographer was able to take a picture of each family together as well as the whole family at once. It was just great. We all worked together, cooked together, cleaned up together, went to the park together, went swimming together.

This past Easter two of my sisters came, my son Sean came, and my daughters came. I just tell everyone, "Come. The house is here." It's not like a commune, but it's a family home that they can all feel they're part of. My nieces and nephews—they're all welcome here, too. Absolutely. My daughter Stephanie and her husband, Adam, right now are living in the little house with their two children.

Sometimes I look back and say, "Well, that wasn't as difficult as I thought it would be." But when you're facing an obstacle, it can seem so enormous. When my husband said he didn't want to be married, it was a shock at first. But then it was like a weight lifted.

I love the story about the two sides of the tapestry. One side has all the knots. That's our life here on earth. We don't know what the other side looks like until we go through all the knots, all the trials and tribulations. But there's a beautiful picture there. Going through the knots, you wonder why. But on the other side, it's like a tapestry.

After my mother died, we found this poem she'd written:

Ode to an Old House
by Faith Castle Conlon

Gallant and brave the old house stood
Silhouetted against the setting sun.
Its weathered face is seamed with age
Like a dreamer whose work is done.

The old house is empty of laughter now.
Silence holds its sway.
Its rooms are waiting for footsteps;
They dream of a bygone day.

Time has given it courage
Along in its twilight years,
Accepting what fate has given it,
Forgotten by those it held dear.

Who said an old house has no soul?
I dare defy their name.
For I have learned that courage
Is greater than worldly gain.

I'm thankful now for all that's happened. I've been given the gift of this house, which I named after my grandmother. Most of all, I've been given the gift of feeling strong enough and confident enough that if there is something I want to do, I know I can do it. I am not alone. I'm no longer afraid. ✐

JOURNAL ENTRY 19

Whereas Mary Orlando revels in having a house filled with loved ones, I enjoy being an empty nester. I adore my children, but my world began revolving around them when I was in my early twenties and remained in that orbit until my youngest son went to college a year ago. Now my days—and nights—are full of glorious possibility!

JOURNAL ENTRY 20

I assume that because I woke up healthy, I'm going to live all day and that tonight I'll be able to climb back into my bed with its blue ticking-striped sheets and stare through my skylight at the stars.

The truth is that a plane could literally fall out of the sky before I even finish writing this page. It could crash into my house and burn me to ashes. There might not even be a body for a funeral. I might just literally disappear. No DNA to track, no teeth to compare with past dental records, no blue plaid pajama bottoms left to identify me. Poof. I'd be gone. And just a nanosecond before, I could have been daydreaming about tomorrow.

I keep asking myself: What am I doing that I want to stop? What am I not doing that I want to begin?

I recently took up scuba diving. My instructor gave me a compass and told me that if I ever got lost, I could use it to swim back to the shore. I used to lament that I had no compass to guide me in my life, no instrument to help me see where I was in relation to where I wanted to be. But I've discovered I was mistaken. My compass is my heart.

JOURNAL ENTRY 21

I first heard about the Ada Comstock Scholars Program at Smith College from an article in a local newspaper about a woman who'd become an "Ada" in her sixties and earned a degree. I decided to contact the program administrator to get some leads on other women late bloomers. Ignoring the butterflies in my stomach (I'm getting better at this), I picked up the phone.

A woman named Sidonia Dalby answered my call. When I told her about my project, she was enthusiastic and supportive. Although she didn't recommend anyone for me to interview, she sent me a book called Textured Lives *celebrating graduates of the program. The night I received it, I sat in bed and read it from cover to cover.*

This is how I learned about Maureen Horkan. Out of all the stories I read that evening, hers resonated the most with me.

"CONCERNING ALL ACTS OF INITIATIVE...
THERE IS ONE ELEMENTARY TRUTH, THE
IGNORANCE OF WHICH KILLS COUNTLESS
IDEAS AND SPLENDID PLANS: THAT THE
MOMENT ONE DEFINITELY COMMITS ONE-
SELF, THEN PROVIDENCE MOVES TOO.
ALL SORTS OF THINGS OCCUR TO HELP
ONE THAT WOULD NEVER OTHERWISE
HAVE OCCURRED."   —Goethe

MAUREEN HORKAN
ASSISTANT STATE ATTORNEY

Barely graduating from high school, Maureen Horkan spent most of her twenties working at a series of low-rung jobs and going from one unsuccessful relationship to another. When the last of her boyfriends became abusive, she decided she'd had enough and resolved to turn her life around. After taking a trip to Greece to celebrate her independence, she embarked on a five-year quest to become an Ada Comstock Scholar at Smith College. Admitted at age thirty, she graduated Phi Beta Kappa three years later and went directly to law school. Today she works as an Assistant State Attorney in Jacksonville, Florida, and is the happily-married mother of a one-year old boy.

Tall, with blue-gray eyes and dark hair, she's joyful and courageous. Projecting both sensitivity and strength, she seems wise beyond her years.

I never knew I loved to learn—how glorious it can be. If you'd asked me in my early twenties if I wanted a free education, I would have turned you down. I didn't even learn how to learn until I was twenty-six years old. And because I didn't know how to succeed, and hated to admit my ignorance, I stifled myself. I felt like I had something to give, but I was afraid to give it.

So if I had to find a place to begin my story, I'd start around fourth grade, because that's when my experience of learning began to change. Up until then, school was fun, and I was very outgoing and joyous. In the mornings I loved leaving my house in Carmel, New York, to go do something exciting.

But then in fourth grade, I started falling behind. My teacher that year was a good man who meant me no harm; but maybe because I was a girl, he expected less of me. We had math relays, for instance, where we would stand in two lines and go up to the board and do a multiplication table. Every time it was my turn, he'd give me the same one. Then he'd wink! To this day, I know six times seven perfectly, but that's literally the only one I can tell you off the top of my head. I didn't learn my multiplication tables, but I got the message that being cute was more important than getting the right answer.

In fifth grade I had another male teacher, and this guy was not nearly as well-intentioned. Since fourth grade had been a year-long beauty pageant and I hadn't learned much, I was now struggling. Looking back, I think I also missed something when I transferred from Catholic school to public school after second grade. I had trouble not only with my times tables but also with spelling and handwriting.

My best friend was in the same class, and the teacher used to tease us. He'd ask one of us a question and tell both of us to put our heads together to figure out the answer. He'd make comments like, "If you two were one person, you might get a C." He was also very flirtatious and would joke that he couldn't live without me. I was tall and skinny, probably my full five-eight by then, and he used to call me "Legs." One day I didn't have time to change out of my shorts after gym class, and he made some comment about my legs, scooped me up and carried me to the nurse's office. He dropped me on the bed and was getting ready to jump on me, when I quickly rolled off to get away from him. The nurse was sitting at her desk right in front of us, clueless. After that, my trust in teachers began to fade. Nobody ever asked why that teacher carried me down the hall and dropped me on the bed, but that was life in the '70s.

Then school started getting harder. By seventh grade, I couldn't keep up. I hated not being able to do the work and started to develop a rebellious spirit. My response to teachers was to be judgmental and disdainful. When I think about it now, it felt like I was missing some important skill or essential know-how necessary to succeed. It felt like I couldn't learn. And to survive that, I had to blame somebody. So it became their fault. They were idiots and school was stupid. By the time I was thirteen, I was getting all D's. I barely graduated from the eighth grade.

On top of this, my family started having money problems. We stayed in Carmel, but we moved five times before I was eighteen. Five of us—my mother, father, one brother, sister and I—ended up in a two-bedroom condo. Luckily, my other brother was in the Navy and he wasn't home very often. Then my parents separated. Talk about distraction. Who could study? My mother might disagree, but I have no memory of ever doing homework after school.

As soon as I was old enough, I became an entrepreneur. I put babysitting flyers on all the mailboxes in our condo community and worked almost every night. I was a great babysitter. The kids loved me.

Then in ninth grade, for some insane reason I thought it would be a great idea to follow my best friend to a Catholic prep school. I was woefully unprepared to be there, which became glaringly obvious once I started getting 65s in every class.

I had already figured out how to survive by being angry. Then I met this guy in my condo community who smoked pot and was an utter delinquent. My first love. The worst boy. Perfect for me.

In school I was unmotivated and unintimidated. I wore jeans every day and got detention all the time. I failed algebra and had to

re-take it in summer school. At my summer parent-teacher conference, it was politely recommended that I not return the next fall.

In tenth grade I went back to Carmel High, the public school. As
soon as I turned sixteen, I started working first as a checker at
Grand Union and then at a department store called Barker's. By
eleventh grade, I was getting out of school at ten o'clock every
morning and going to work. High school was just this funny blip at
the beginning of the day. Although I remember being encouraged
by a few teachers who said I was bright, they couldn't convince me.
I just thought they didn't know how stupid I was. I barely passed
most of my classes.

Even though I'd been beaten down intellectually, I was very
creative and motivated to succeed at something. One summer
when I was only fifteen or sixteen, I signed up for a program in
fashion design for high school students at Parsons School of Design
in New York City. I paid for the course with my own money and
rode the train into the city every Saturday for a couple of months.
My dad taught me the path to walk the six or eight blocks from
Grand Central to the school. At the end of the program I got a
little certificate. I was so proud of myself.

By the time I was eighteen, I'd been promoted to assistant manager of the ladies department at Barker's and had saved up four
thousand dollars. The job at Barker's, the course at Parsons and the
motivation to do something with my life shifted my focus enough
to think about leaving home. I couldn't wait to be on my own.

After I graduated, I took out a student loan and went to the Art
Institute of Ft. Lauderdale, which I discovered at the back of a
fashion magazine. I'd been freezing for all of my young life. If you
wanted to look good in Carmel, you did not dress warm. Florida
sounded wonderful to me.

Nobody in my family had ever gone to college. My mother was
a stay-at-home mom who worked part-time, and my dad was an

air conditioning contractor. Still, this was the sort of college—a trade college—that seemed within my grasp. I would never have thought to go to an academic college. No one suggested it, no one offered to pay for it, and I surely didn't have the grades.

I remember the day I left New York. It was December 29th, and I was eighteen years old. I'd never been on a plane before, and I was so disappointed when I got an aisle seat. But it was a thrill to fly and a revelation to get away. Maybe that's why I later became a flight attendant.

To my surprise, I did really well in fashion school. I learned all about the history of fashion, the history of clothes. Truthfully, I don't know how I studied it all, but I did. I probably did well because I was enjoying myself and getting positive feedback. (Not one of my teachers felt compelled to comment on my legs!) It was the first time this had ever happened to me. I was a star student and popular with the professors. I even won awards. But at the same time, even though I was succeeding academically, going to school felt like such an indulgent waste of time because I wasn't making any money. "This is insane," I thought. "I need to be working." I had no concept of the value of education. My thinking was, "I'm getting all A's; I completely know what they're talking about; I don't need to go to school for this; I don't need a degree."

Plus, I have to say that I was homesick. Leaving my sister in Carmel, I thought my heart would fall out of my chest, and I missed my mom. Also, right before I went to Ft. Lauderdale, I'd fallen in love.

Within four or five months, my boyfriend came to live with me in Florida. My own restlessness was compounded by his, and the two of us ended up moving back to New York at the end of my spring semester. I already felt I should be working instead of going to school, and it didn't take much for him to convince me to drop out.

Immediately I started working in retail again. I got a job as the assistant manager of a ladies' clothing shop making something like $4.50 an hour. Here I was thinking it was a waste of money to be in college, and what did I do? I came back to Carmel and started working in this store for pennies, dressing mannequins and selling shirts.

There was always this drive in me to compensate for the fact that my family struggled financially. It was a huge deal for me to be able to provide for myself. So on a whim, I ended up quitting and applying for a position as a layout designer/draftsperson for an IBM subcontracting firm. I had no experience with blueprints. None at all. But on my resume, I'd written, "Drafted floor plan layouts for merchandising," which was true. I'd also put down that I'd been to fashion school and had taken the course at Parsons. The guy doing the hiring liked me and must have been desperate because he gave me the job. All of a sudden, I doubled my income.

After a year, though, I decided it had been a crazy idea to come home and that I wanted to go back to Florida. It was freezing in New York. So my boyfriend and I and another friend all moved to Ft. Lauderdale, and eventually my sister joined us. We had a four-bedroom house on the water and were like a family. I got a job designing fashion displays, but once again I was making very little money. After a year or so, I became a waitress and then eventually a bartender. I was finally cranking in the cash.

I must have been looking for more adventure, though, because then I met this older Frenchman named Eric who was just entirely too appealing for me not to run off with. I was twenty-three, and he was thirty. He was stern and very serious, and all of a sudden I had this controlling boyfriend. (Of course, I didn't think of him as "controlling" back then. I just thought he was smart and strong.) He lived on a sailboat; and because he was into boats, I became interested in boats. He got me a job preparing a charter sailboat to be delivered to the Virgin Islands. I helped sand, shellac and clean every surface.

Then I was asked to be crew. I thought, "Oh my God, this must be a dream." I had my own cabin because I was the only girl on board, and I slept like a baby. I remember sailing into one port where the water was clear blue. You could see right to the sandy bottom and see hundreds of starfish lying there. At one point, the guys put me in one of the sails and hung it down the side of the boat. Just incredible; I'll never forget it. That's when I started keeping a journal. I knew my life was changing. I'd fallen in love; I felt poetic; I had something to say.

After my sailing adventure, Eric decided to move back to France and wanted me to go with him. He didn't have to ask me twice. I really think I wanted to be French. I said goodbye to my little Florida family and ran away to Paris.

What an incredible experience France was for me! I just couldn't get over the food, the music, the buildings. I had grown up in Carmel, New York where the oldest thing was the court-house. I became so aware that there was a whole other world out there. The dishes, the linens, the Coca-Colas in pretty bottles—I loved all of it. Even the butter was a thrill. I thought, "Where did they get this? This is butter?" It tasted as though it came right out of the cow. And in the morning, there were these little pastries with the most delicious jams and jellies.

Being in France made me aware of my ignorance. I was exposed to a level of culture that I hadn't really thought about before. Eric's family had money and was educated. He was much more cultured than I was. And, although he was often verbally abusive, his taunt-ing challenged me intellectually. He told me I was smart and that I could learn. He tried to get me up to speed, or at least to encour-age me to want to be up to speed. In Ft. Lauderdale, he worked on boats, but he was really an engineer and very good at math.

When he realized that I didn't know my multiplication tables, he began spontaneously—and rudely—quizzing me in the middle of our conversations.

While I was in France, I also began reading. There was no shower in our Paris apartment, and I learned to love taking deep, luxurious baths. My mother had given me Anne Morrow Lindbergh's *A Gift From the Sea,* and I found myself slowly reading passages aloud over and over again as I bathed each day. I tell you, that book really grabbed me. I was in awe of Lindbergh's writing. Growing up, I didn't read at all. I never read a thing in high school. At some point, I'd read *Little House on the Prairie,* but it wasn't beautiful. What struck me about Anne Morrow Lindbergh's book was that it was beautiful. I was just stunned by the sounds, the truth, the eloquence.

So France was a real wake-up call for me. At the time, maybe because of my lack of maturity, I wasn't able to totally devour the experience. But the combination of the classical music, the food and Anne Morrow Lindberg in the bathtub really affected me.

Unfortunately, almost as soon as we got to Paris, Eric went off on a tangent. He found some electronic boat equipment product that he wanted to import to the United States and suddenly informed me that we were moving back to Ft. Lauderdale.

I was so upset. I was ready to stay and learn French. I wanted to do more, see more. I hadn't hurried myself along and done anything. "Why did I need to visit the Eiffel Tower and the Louvre right away when I was living in Paris?" I reasoned.

As soon as we moved back to Florida, I started to waitress again. Eric didn't have money, and he wanted to start an import business. He literally got off the boat with his toiletries bag and moved into my house. I paid all the bills and paid for the apartment. Everything in the place was mine; I'd had it all before. So here I was, this twenty-three-year-old supporting a thirty-year-old man.

Then I started noticing that Eric was drinking a lot. I'd sort of missed this before. Cokes with double shots of vodka during the day; Heinekens at night. He smelled terrible. He also started getting more abusive. I suppose he needed to put me down to feel better about himself. So I had to curb myself a lot and "behave" to keep from incurring his wrath.

But the flip side of our relationship is that Eric pushed me to do more with my life. He kept telling me I shouldn't just be a waitress. Going to France had awakened a desire in me to travel, so I decided to become a flight attendant. I applied to different airlines, filled out the paperwork and went through the interview process for each one. I eventually got hired by Eastern Airlines, which was based in Miami, right down the road from Ft. Lauderdale. It was quite an achievement for me. Soon after, I told Eric I was moving out. I couldn't take the abusive stuff anymore.

Right away, I got myself a little cottage. I'd left home seven years earlier and had never been on my own without a live-in boyfriend. Wanting to figure out how not to have a partner, I bought a beautiful white wrought iron single daybed. It was a huge deal for me. Very expensive. I kept waiting and waiting for the bill, but, incredibly, the bill never came. I've always thought this was God's way of approving my plan to be single for a while.

Still, I couldn't quite leave the relationship. I kept getting pulled back. This went on for more than a year. The biggest problem was that Eric didn't want me to leave, and, to keep me tied to him, he wouldn't let me take my stuff. But I'd worked very hard to have a home, and I wanted my things back, most of which I'd had before Eric and I moved in together.

Finally Eric agreed that I could come and get my belongings. So I borrowed a truck for the day and took my sister with me. (God knows why I brought my eighty-pound sister instead of someone with a badge and a weapon!) We got almost everything out of the house, but Eric wouldn't let me take my drafting table. I refused to leave without it. When I went to get it, he grabbed me and tried to drag me away from it. My sister came to my rescue, but he threw her across the room. Then he threw me out the front door. I bounded back, punched him in the face and shoved past him. I went again to get it. He followed me. We were both tugging on the table when one of the detachable metal legs came off in my hand. I grabbed that piece of hard metal and said, "I'm gonna hit you if you don't let go of that desk." If he hadn't let go, I really think I would have hit him. I would have taken every ounce of rage from every mean teacher I'd ever had and every abusive man I'd ever been with and smacked him in the head with that thing.

He looked at me, and he knew. He knew I was going to hit him. It was an intense moment. We were eye to eye, and he saw there was no way I was going to relent.

I threw the desk in the back of the truck and drove away. I cried tears I'd never cried before, made noises I'd never heard myself make. My heart had broken wide open. I'd done this all alone, had fought for what was mine. That desk symbolized something to me—the creative person that got that damn layout designer job in New York. I was taking that person back!

On the anniversary of living alone for one year, I bought an atlas and wrote in it, "Dear Maureen: You can do whatever you want. You can go wherever you want." I realized that part of my attachment to Eric had been my quest for a more exciting life, and I knew I had to find a way to do that for myself.

So in celebration of my one-year anniversary of being alone, I decided to travel to somewhere I wanted to go. I planned a month-long trip to Greece. Even though several of my flight-attendant friends would have loved to have traveled with me, I wanted to go alone.

I didn't want to have any fear about traveling by myself, so I prepared for the trip by going to the library. I took out all these books on Greece—tour books and history books—and ended up stumbling across all this Greek mythology and goddess stuff. It was a delicious year. The Ft. Lauderdale library was just wonderful. I'd never really gone to a library before. After a while, it was all I wanted to do in my spare time.

Planning for Greece took about six months. Then I discovered other things in the library stacks, like literature and autobiography. That's when I started reading women writers. I would just take books off the shelves and sit on the floor and cry as I read. It was validating and comforting to read about these women's lives and find in them reflections of my own.

As a result of being in the library, I began to think about school. I was reading. I was writing. I was starving to learn.

Then my good friend Frances, one of the angels in my life, said to me, "Why don't you check out Smith College in Northampton, Massachusetts? I think you'd like it." I'd never heard of Smith College before. If I had heard about it, I would have been intimidated.

At first I dismissed the whole thing as a silly idea. It still felt indulgent to go to college. I thought my family would think I was crazy. It didn't take much to muffle me; I had so many fears about my own intellect. And even though I later learned that the Ada Comstock program at Smith is geared toward non-traditional students, I felt too old to be starting school. But since I was already in the library, I thought, why not at least look at the catalogue for fun?

In the catalogue I read excerpts from Sophia Smith's will. She's the founder of Smith, and in her will, she sets out her mission statement for the college. It was an incredible thing for me to read —a woman-to-woman epiphany. It didn't feel like reading a catalogue. Instead it was as if I had opened a personal letter written just for me. I felt spoken to. These were her words. And it was her school. And it was for me, for women like me.

What I read is that Smith helps women to become whole, to feel useful and meaningful and valuable in society, and to give back whatever they have to give. That's what I needed to hear. It was saying, "Come. Be fed. Let yourself listen to and think about the writings of others." Anne Morrow Lindbergh had gone there. Sylvia Plath had gone there. I thought, "Oh my God, how can I go there?"

I had to go there. That was it. I had to go find this place. It really touched me. It was like God spoke through Sophia and said, "Maureen, you have a place in this world. You are not useless. You have talent. You are brilliant. You've been squashing yourself. You should go and do what you really want to do. I have faith in you." That's what I felt sitting there in the library.

I read the catalogue right before my trip to Greece and decided I had to go check this place out before I left. This was in October of 1987. So I flew into Bradley International Airport in Hartford and rented a car. I stayed at the Autumn Inn, a fabulous bed and breakfast right down the road from the college.

I just went to look and to let myself feel what it would be like to go to such a place. I didn't have a tour. I didn't tell anyone I was there. I'd barely gotten a high school diploma. Smith seemed way out of my league. But, still, I had to see it.

When I arrived, I couldn't believe how beautiful it was, how at home I felt. I was so moved by the space. The buildings were old and gracious; the dorms looked like palaces.

From my study of Greece and from my time in France, I'd become so tuned in to feeling the history of things, the legacy of things. I was also aware of all the famous women who had gone to Smith. And as I sat there on the lawn and watched women walking by, I thought, "My God, do they have any idea where they are?

Do they know that the rest of us are out here slugging hash and putting up with groping men and serving cocktails and calculating the price of beer? Do they have any idea where their sisters are?"

I was really out of the fold and looking for safe female spaces. I felt it right away, that this was a safe space for women. Women even looked different there. There was a sense of beauty that wasn't commercialized.

Before I left that day, I went to the school bookstore and bought a Smith T-shirt, a Smith pencil and some other memorabilia. Then I went on my trip.

My month-long visit to Greece was cathartic. It's one thing to tell yourself you can do anything you want and another to go do it and have a blessed experience besides. Even the language barrier wasn't much of a problem. I found people to help me at every stage.

I hadn't picked any hotels in advance, and I didn't have any reservations. All I had was a backpack and a plane ticket. But I was really comfortable when I got there because I'd done all the research.

I stayed in Athens about a week. Then I took a boat to Santorini. Even though I had plans to keep going, once I got there, I didn't want to leave. I rode a moped all over the island. It was the most magical place I'd ever been. My room cost maybe twelve dollars. It was just this little cave embedded in a hillside. And the guy who owned the place, along with a friend of his, took me out to dinner and dancing. They were such gentlemen. For the most part, though, I was quiet. I wrote in my journal and just enjoyed myself. When I left, I felt I'd achieved what I went to achieve. It was a long, quiet meditation—my own coming of age.

Back in Florida, I continued going to the library. I read Ibsen and Chekhov. Then, with the idea of someday applying to Smith, I enrolled at Broward Community College in Ft. Lauderdale. Before registering for classes, though, I had to take a placement exam. It was a painful experience. I scored really low, which was demoralizing, and had to start at the very beginning. I'd still never learned how to learn.

I began with one night class: How to write a sentence. It was very remedial, and I did okay. But by the time I got to a regular English course, I'm telling you, I was really struggling. My grammar was atrocious. I didn't know where to put a comma, didn't know how to capitalize, didn't know how to spell. Topic sentences? I didn't understand the concept at all. My writing was very flowery. I had no sense of power, no sense of how to articulate with strength. Every essay I wrote during the first few weeks was returned with the word "rewrite" on top. I was devastated. Over and over again, my teacher sent me back to the drawing board.

Finally, I decided to write the most boring piece I could imagine. The essay was called "How to Build a Quilt." It was like an instruction manual. I took out all the adjectives and simplified everything. It was so basic, but I got an A. Thanks to that miserable class and that teacher, who at the time I despised, I eventually learned how to do college writing. She used to tell us that once we mastered the basics, we would have the building blocks for creativity; and she was right. I ended up learning all that stuff—grammar, punctuation, how to write topic sentences—with a vengeance.

The real thrill for me, though, was my literature classes. They were pure bliss. I was the student you dream of; I read everything twice! I remember taking a course where we read six novels in one semester: Brontë, Dickens, George Eliot and a few more. I felt expanded by the stories as I read the words out loud alone in my little carriage house. I spent hours upon hours reading in my favorite chair. Just delicious. It may not sound like anything special to anyone else, but to me, who rarely sat anywhere for any length of time, this was pure luxury. I had been working since I was fourteen years old; and for this over-tired, undereducated "worker-bee," a literature class was a veritable million-dollar birthday gift.

The biggest problem was making time to take courses. I was still a flight attendant and on-call with a pager. I had to bid to get my days off, and this was all done by computer. The computer couldn't care less whether I had a class. At first I only needed Monday night, and I always managed to get it. But after I added Tuesday, there was no way the computer would give me two days off in a row every week.

I knew I had to stop flying, but it was so hard to give up my job. I loved being a flight attendant. I got free tickets for my parents and myself, and my schedule was really flexible. So that was the first hurdle I had to surmount. But wanting to go to Smith College was more important than free tickets, so I took a lot of deep breaths and just quit.

I got a nine-to-five job as an accounts payable clerk. I hated it and still only managed to take two courses, one of which I failed. Pre-algebra. It was terrible. I was right back at the beginning again with a teacher who I couldn't understand. I almost gave up.

Then I went and spoke with a school counselor about becoming a full-time student. I knew I needed to go full-time, and I knew I needed a different job. She helped me with some loan paperwork and also helped me write up a scholarship application. I think I got two thousand dollars, which wasn't much, but it was something.

The counselor also advised me that some of the best teachers taught during the day, and she recommended a math teacher named Mrs. Anderson. I ended up taking this woman for every level of math I could because she was so clear and precise. She's the one who taught me how to learn. She made a huge difference for me in terms of being able to feel confident and keep going.

Later, with another teacher, I even took calculus. After I discovered that I wasn't as stupid as I had been taught to believe,

I was fueled by resentment. "Don't tell me I can't do this!" It was like going to war with a shield and a sword. I'm a math survivor!

Honestly, it was rather awesome to discover how simple the learning process was. It was not obscure or intangible or reserved for smart people. It just took good old-fashioned hard work. Clearly, I had worked hard in fashion school and had done well, but I never put two and two together to see that I was using academic skills. Once I realized that learning was something I could accomplish—if I could just calm my mind down enough to relax and start at the beginning—I began getting A's on my exams. And each one was proof that I was not stupid, that I was not missing anything. Each one was a private victory march.

Anyway, I finally quit my position as an accounts payable clerk and got a job as a waitress at Houston's in Ft. Lauderdale. I worked there for four years and eventually made enough money to be a full-time student. But at first, all they could guarantee me was three lunch shifts, which was only about a hundred-and-fifty to two hundred dollars a week. I owed four-hundred-and-fifty dollars a month for rent and had all these other bills to pay on a regular basis. So my bills and my income didn't match. But I believed it was the right restaurant, and I believed it would work out. I didn't care if it was going to be difficult. I figured if I had to eat peanut butter, I would eat peanut butter; but I was going to be a full-time student in the fall, and I was going to work at Houston's.

And it did work out. I'd get an extra shift just when I needed the money. One day, I remember I didn't have enough to pay my rent, which was just horrifying to me. I couldn't believe that I'd done this, that I'd made this choice and now I couldn't pay my rent. I was so mad at God. I said, "I gave up my job, and I stopped being a flight attendant, and I knew this was the right thing to do, and I need the money right now!" And I went to the mailbox and there was a check for a hundred dollars, a Christmas bonus from my church for Sunday school teaching.

Along the way, I got lots of other little reminders telling me I was on the right track. Driving to class the very first night, I became aware that there was a little blue VW Beetle in front of me. I've always driven Volkswagens. To me, it's my car. Very symbolic. Anyway, every time the traffic slowed down, the Beetle would pull away; but I'd still see it ahead of me in the distance. Then, when I got to the last traffic light before taking a left into the school, I pulled right up to it. It had a Smith College bumper sticker! No one in Ft. Lauderdale knew what I was talking about when I said I wanted to go to Smith. "Who is he?" they'd say. Or "Smith what?" And here was this little blue Volkswagen on my very first night of school with a Smith College bumper sticker.

So many times I'd be panicking about something—I'm not smart enough to do this; I don't have enough money—and I would look up and there would be an advertisement for somebody running for office. It would just say, "Smith." Little things like that kept me going.

I also got a lot of encouragement from my friends and family. Someone bought me flash cards as a gift. I found them on my car one day. And my brother gave me a check for my first course. I was so touched. Then his wife made me a badge of courage, a round cloth medallion hanging from a red ribbon that literally said "Courage" on it. I wore it under my clothing for every single exam of my academic career. (I also used my Smith pencil for every exam. It's just a stub now, but you can still see the word "Smith" printed on it.)

Then, when I felt like I was ready, after I'd gone full-time for a year and a half, I applied to Smith. On paper I looked good. I'd volunteered at my church. I'd been successful at work. I'd also taken several honors courses and had a 3.8 overall average. My academic record was great. I thought I'd be number one on Smith's admit list. Hey, I saw a Smith bumper sticker on the first day of school. I've been invited. You couldn't convince me otherwise.

I felt so sure I was going that I'd packed up my little cottage, put everything in storage and moved into my sister's apartment— even though it was really hard to leave the home I'd created. I kept waiting and waiting for my acceptance letter, but it never came. Finally, I called the college and asked them if they'd made a decision. The person on the phone said, "I'm sorry to tell you, but you've been declined."

I couldn't believe it. I thought they'd made a mistake. I'd taken five levels of math and had gotten five A's. For two weeks I just sat in a chair that I bought for five dollars at the Salvation Army. I call it my depression chair. I could barely go to work. I couldn't do anything. Thank God the semester was over. On top of it all, I had to tell everyone that I'd been turned down.

The whole thing was a spiritual crisis for me. How could anyone miss the bumper sticker and the signposts? I'd had such confidence in my fate. I mean, some people hope for a gold medal and don't get it, but this was different. People can go to Smith, and I should have been one of them.

So I took the summer off, moved into a new place and regrouped. I got a grip on myself. I think I knew right away I wasn't going to give up; I knew I was going to reapply. But I needed to experience the fallout.

The next semester I redoubled my efforts and signed up for five honors courses. I decided to get my associate's and apply again with a completed degree. I was defiant: You just see if you can turn me down next year. You just wait! That's how I felt.

So I finished up the year and applied again. This time I got an envelope with a *yes* inside. It was an incredible experience. I'll never forget it. I fell to the floor; I couldn't get up. I called everybody from that position. I was so happy. It seemed like everything led up to this one moment.

Then I got a second letter saying I'd been awarded a nineteen-thousand-dollar grant. I was like, "Holy cow!" I hadn't been thinking about the money thing. Even back when I was a flight attendant, people would laugh when I'd tell them I wanted to go to Smith. They'd say, "Do you know how much that costs?" But it said in the catalogue, "If you are accepted, the means will be provided." (They used to have a need-blind admissions policy, but sadly they don't anymore.) I repeated that over and over again. It was not my business to figure out how I would pay for it. All I had to do was get in.

Before I left for Northampton, I packed all the things I wanted to take. Everything else I just left where it was. Then I invited all my friends over and put out a box that said, "Donations." I didn't want to have a tag sale and put my stuff out on the street, but I could let my friends take it all. Even if they gave me nothing, I didn't care. It so happens, though, that I made around fifteen hundred dollars. My church also took up a donation and gave me a couple thousand dollars. Then my dear friend Phyllis and her husband threw me a fabulous graduation party. It was such a worthy send-off.

At Smith, I was assigned to a traditional student dorm. The idea that someone was going to cook three meals a day for me was phenomenal. I couldn't wait. I just wanted a room and dinner. After five years at community college, I was pooped.

I lived on the fifth floor of Northrup House. The first four floors housed traditional-aged students, some as young as seventeen. The fifth floor was the attic, with six small rooms and a bathroom. These were for the Ada's. The room next to mine was vacant. There was a name on the door, but the person never showed. Later, I found out why.

That first night I went to Convocation. It's a big event where the auditorium is just filled with women and jamming with energy. I felt old and out of place. I'm the kind of person who always seeks an aisle seat. Always. But when I sat down on the aisle, I just wasn't comfortable. I can't explain it. So I got up, turned around and saw another empty place in the middle of a row next to a woman who looked about my age. I asked her if that seat was taken, and she said no.

Her name was Cathy, and it turns out that she was the person who hadn't shown up at the dorm. She'd chickened out and gotten an apartment. She became my dearest friend at Smith, and she wouldn't have been there the year before if I'd gotten in when I first applied. I needed to wait for Cathy to get there!

Also, if I hadn't changed my seat, we wouldn't have met right away. We might have met down the road, but this way we met the very first night. We were the closest of friends for all three years. I wouldn't have had the same experience at Smith without her.

The other bit of symmetry that happened has to do with the fact that I call God "Grace." It's amazing how one word can end up being a touchstone for your whole life. That's the way the word grace is for me. Just hearing the word causes me to exhale and relax. It means I am loved and I am not alone. During the period when I was leaving Eric, renting the carriage house and living on my own for the first time, I remember realizing how very small and misdirected I felt at the heart of my life. And it was somehow easier to deal with all of that when I was in my car. I love to drive the same way I love to fly. Motion, the idea of taking off, has always been freeing and exciting and some sort of esoteric relief for me. Anyway, one day I was in my car, crying and driving and feeling so wounded when I began to have this awesome sense that I was not alone, that there was a presence in the car with me. It sounds sappy; but I'm telling you, I was not alone in that car. And the more I trusted in my life, and the more open I was, the more I found this loving Grace all around me. The little miracles were everywhere, like the Smith College bumper sticker and the bonus check when I ran out of money. But there was so much more. The things I would read, the people I would meet on any given day—just everything seemed infused with it. These mysterious acts and events, these are the threads—the deepest truth—of my life. They are the stitches that hold the rest of it together and give it strength and meaning.

Anyway, when I got to Smith and walked into the dorm, standing there was this beautiful girl. She said, "Welcome. My name is Grace." I laughed and smiled and thought to myself, of course it is!

This kind of symmetry was a regular occurrence while I was at Smith. In fact, the phrase "Guess what?" became a little joke between my friend Cathy and me. Every time we got together, I seemed to have another "Guess what?" story to tell, some amazing thing, some perfect synchronicity that, according to her, would only happen to me.

The final "Guess what?" happened right before graduation. I got a letter asking me to thank the donor who was responsible for the bulk of my Smith education. And guess who it was? Anne Morrow Lindbergh's father! From my literary awakening in that tub in France to my graduation—now isn't that just over the top? Of course, I nearly passed out when I read it.

I made it through Smith with flying colors. I was prepared academically and never felt stupid there; I was blessed by the process. In 1995, at the age of thirty-three, I graduated Phi Beta Kappa with a BA in English, eight years after taking those first literature courses in Ft. Lauderdale.

The luxury of the learning environment at Smith was even more decadent than at the community college. The reading was glorious; the conversations were profound. The sheer solitude and beauty was worth everything I gave up, every penny I paid, to get there. It's my intention to have my ashes spread on the ground there when I die. It would be heaven to me, to be on that campus again.

I could have easily gone forward in English and become a professor. But I had been on the student-run judicial board at Smith, and I couldn't ignore the fact that I had an advocate's voice. Even when I tried really hard not to influence people, I was persuasive. And even if I tried to hold myself down, I would still lead. I thought, "I have to follow the truth of that," and I believed that the legal profession would be the right place for my talents. It was a harsh call considering my academic history, but I had to go with it. So, in my senior year I applied to law school and got into Florida State, which is in Tallahassee. I was accepted to a couple of others, but Florida still felt like my home.

Honestly, law school was awful. I dropped into an utter patriarchy, a boys' club. It took me right back to the beginning, to that kid being called "Legs" and being asked what six times seven is. But I refused to give up. I graduated at the age of thirty-six. When I took the Bar exam, I wore the badge of courage my sister-in-law had made for me when I started at the community college, but this time I wore it on the outside of my clothes!

For the past five years I've been a prosecutor with the State Attorney's Office in Jacksonville. I prosecute cases of domestic violence against children. It's really an honor and a blessing to stand up for these victims. Many of my own experiences—some of which I've shared with you and some of which I've chosen to leave out—help me relate deeply to these children and to advocate for them with understanding and compassion.

I am also married to a wonderful man I met in law school. And while I often wonder why I decided to be a lawyer with all the stress that goes along with the job, I always conclude that God had to make sure I met Jason. He keeps me laughing and spontaneously dancing in the living room, and he forces me to goof off far more than I ever would without him.

Truthfully, I'm still feeling out where I belong in the legal world. My son, Michael, was born a year ago, and I'm not sure if I want to keep doing what I'm doing now. But I have faith in myself. Fulfilling my dream of going to Smith taught me so much about my ability to make things happen in my life. It was an unfathomable goal, considering my skills and my lack of money and resources. The desire to go just grew like a root inside my soul and became stronger and stronger. It was an absolute, clear unmistakable intention. I felt unstoppable, and I was. Nothing deterred me. What a lesson! What a thing to learn, that you can will yourself into the reality of your choice. I left Smith with my full self, and I've been able to keep that through everything I've done.

My story hasn't ended yet. There is no end to dreaming. But once you figure out how to do something like this, you can do anything. ✑

JOURNAL ENTRY 22

The book is not yet finished, but it's already been rejected by fourteen publishers. (I started to say, "I've been rejected," but that's not strictly the case.) Two weeks ago, I thought it was going to be picked up by a smaller imprint. Now, after an initial flurry of hopeful e-mails, it looks as though it might have been turned down by that publisher as well.

Throughout this period, I've been working on Maureen Horkan's story. It's as if her spirit is with me, urging me onward with that sword and shield she used to battle her math demons. I keep thinking, if she could continue to march toward her dream in the face of being declined by Smith after five years of community college, I shouldn't let myself lose heart after a mere fifteen rejections.

JOURNAL ENTRY 23

My heaven-sent agent Paul Fedorko called today and said he's finally found a publisher for the book. The perfect one. I'm positively giddy.

JOURNAL ENTRY 24

Eighteen months ago I saw Jean Karotkin's photographs in Rosie magazine and was so touched by her images of breast cancer survivors that I cut out the six-page spread and saved it in a manila folder. But until Richard Hunt told me about her last week—he's publishing her book as well as mine—and suggested I might want to interview her, I had no idea that Jean was the one who took these exquisite photographs and that she herself is a late bloomer.

"RISK! RISK ANYTHING! CARE NO MORE
FOR THE OPINIONS OF OTHERS, FOR THOSE
VOICES. DO THE HARDEST THING ON EARTH
FOR YOU. ACT FOR YOURSELF."

—Katherine Mansfield

JEAN KAROTKIN
PHOTOGRAPHER

After being diagnosed at age thirty-eight with breast cancer and undergoing a mastectomy, Jean Karotkin was given a clean bill of health. Hearing the good news as a wake-up call, she left a difficult marriage, designed a new home for herself and began to dream of publishing a book of photographs of breast cancer survivors—even though she'd never taken a professional photograph. Twelve years later, she was exhibiting her black-and-white images at the prestigious Houston Center for Photography and having her work featured in *Oprah* and *Rosie* magazines. Her book, aptly titled *Body & Soul,* is coming out in 2004.

With delicate features, dark hair and penetrating eyes, she's every bit as beautiful—both inside and out—as the women she captures on film.

I always tell people that my life began when I was diagnosed with breast cancer. In retrospect, though, I can see that everything that has happened to me has been for a purpose, and that from the time I was a young girl I've been on a journey to get where I am today.

I grew up in Dallas, Texas, and, honestly, I don't remember much about my childhood. I do have wonderful memories, though, of seventh grade. I had a great group of friends and even a boyfriend. But then, in the summer before eighth grade, my whole world changed.

Just as I was getting ready to enter junior high and a brand new school, I started wearing a brace to treat scoliosis—which is a curvature of the spine. The brace had a solid, very heavy leather girdle about one-half- to three-quarters-of-an-inch thick that extended from the bottom of my ribs down to where my leg and hip were connected. It was fitted to my body. Attached to this leather piece was a single, shiny heavy metal bar that went up to a moon-shaped chin rest.

While new cliques were forming and other girls were trying out for cheerleading and the drill team, I was in this metal contraption. For three years, from eighth grade through tenth grade, I wore the brace all the time and was unable to do any physical activity. People stared at me, and I lost friends. No one wanted to sit next to me. I didn't go to parties and didn't get asked to dance. My life shut down.

Yet as painful as it was, wearing this brace had two positive effects on my life. First, it gave me great empathy toward people who have disabilities. I developed a sensitivity. And as I sat at the top of the bleachers and watched the world go by, I also became an observer.

Following high school, I attended the University of Oklahoma and graduated with a degree in arts and sciences. Then at age twenty-one, I got married. The marriage was incredibly difficult for me. Of course, I went into it with very low self-esteem. I didn't know how to speak up for myself or how to make decisions on my own. I had no voice.

I was married seven years before my daughter, Suzanne, was born. During that time, I worked in retail. Like many women, I wanted to be productive outside the home and was searching to find an identity for myself. So when Suzanne turned three, I tried going back to work again. I ended up choosing to be a full-time mother instead. Taking care of my child—this daughter I adore, this gift—was the most important thing to me.

Then when Suzanne was eleven, I went for a baseline mammogram. I was thirty-eight years old. My mother had had breast cancer, and she'd been urging me to get a check-up. But because I'd never met anyone as young as I was who'd been diagnosed, and because I was flat, I thought there was no way I would ever get cancer. That's what everyone thinks.

After my check-up, the doctor said, "You look great; everything looks fine. We'll just wait for the lab results." Four days later I got a phone call from her. She said, "We found some calcifications—small calcium deposits in the breast tissue—that might indicate something suspicious. I want to direct you to a surgeon." I remember the moment so clearly. It was late afternoon, and I was sitting on my bedroom floor.

This was in October of 1988, right before the Jewish holidays, and I was planning a trip to New York with my parents. I didn't tell them about my mammogram results. I didn't tell anybody. I wanted to get more information first. Although I'd gotten a second opinion, I wasn't sure what I should do.

In desperate need of girl talk, I decided one morning to call my friend Lisa. I hadn't seen her for a while and thought I'd ask her if she wanted to meet me for lunch. Unable to get ahold of her, I went to the restaurant by myself. When I walked in, there she was, sitting alone! She said, "Come join me and tell me what's going on in your life." So I sat down and started telling her about the mammogram. "Hold everything," she said. "I'm going to make a phone call."

In a roundabout fashion, Lisa put me in touch with a prominent breast surgeon at Baylor University Hospital in Dallas. I made an appointment and, I'm telling you, I spent five minutes with him and immediately knew that this was the right guy for me. He gave me information; he gave me choices. I also loved his bedside manner. All of this was so important to me. He said, "Take the trip with your parents to New York. If there's a malignancy, it's only in the beginning stages and it's slow-growing."

I went to New York, carrying my fear with me. When I returned to Dallas, I had the biopsy. My childhood friend Debbie came with me and was stroking my forehead and holding my hand as the anesthetic was wearing off. The doctor was very blunt. He said, "It's malignant."

The surgery was scheduled for ten days later, for the 19th of November—just a few days before my daughter's birthday. I had an early birthday party for her, bought and wrapped all the Christmas gifts and tried to put my affairs in order. I really thought I was going to die.

The night before the surgery, I went into the hospital. I'd elected to have breast reconstruction, and that evening both the plastic surgeon and the breast surgeon marked my body up like a road map. The next morning I had a bilateral mastectomy of my left breast and reconstruction. When I returned to my hospital room from recovery, two of my Houston friends, Edna and Eva, were there to be with me.

My tumor, it turns out, was very, very small—the size of a pin-head. It was self-contained, and a subsequent biopsy showed that my lymph nodes were clean. Both my surgeon and my oncologist agreed that no further treatment—neither chemotherapy nor radiation—was necessary.

I took this news and thought, "Okay, I have a job to do." I forgot about dying and went home and started planning for the future. I got this sense of urgency that I needed to start making things happen in my life. I needed to start living.

The first thing I did after recovering from the surgery was to start a chocolate business. Before I was diagnosed, my friend Debbie and I had been discussing the idea of doing this. She had visited New York and seen a little mom-and-pop candy store that sold chocolate and molds for making chocolate suckers. The owners also did birthday parties for children where kids made chocolate themselves. We thought, "Oh man, there's nothing like that here in Dallas," and we wanted to do something similar. Everything just fell into place. We opened our store in April of '89 and called it "Surprises!"

The day before we opened the business, I made the decision to end my marriage. The cancer gave me the strength and the will to do it. I felt like the cancer was saying to me, "You'd better make changes now. Life is very precious."

The chocolate business got me through the divorce. It came at just the right time and was great therapy. Debbie and I had the store almost three years. After we sold the business, I decided to get out of the house I'd been in during my marriage.

I wanted to relocate to a neighborhood with people sitting outside on front porches and where there were other children for Suzanne to play with. I wanted my daughter to have a sense of community, which was something lacking in our old neighborhood. I looked around, but couldn't find anything I liked. So I built a house from scratch—the same one I live in now. It was a new beginning for my daughter and me. I designed it myself. We broke ground in July of 1993 and were in the house the following March. It's a soft contemporary—open, with lots of light.

A month after we broke ground, I was reading the newspaper one Sunday morning when I saw a self-portrait of a Russian activist/artist on the front cover of the *New York Times* magazine. The woman's face, the structure of it, was so beautiful. A white gauze scarf was tied around her head, and she wore a white body-sculpting dress. From the waist up, the right side of her dress had been cut away to expose her right shoulder, right arm and her mastectomy scar.

The image was about beauty and sexuality and how we view ourselves. I thought, "Wait a minute. I want other people to see this, to be able to see what I see when I look at this photograph." In our society, we have this whole misconception of what beauty is. If we lose a breast, does that mean we're not beautiful, that we're not sexual, that we're not feminine? No.

Right then I came up with the idea of getting top photographers to photograph other women who have had mastectomies. I started creating a whole vision of doing a book. I didn't have the confidence or the skill at that point to do it myself, but I had the vision.

Suzanne by then was in high school, and I knew that she'd be going away to college in a few years. So once we were settled in the new house, I started thinking, "Okay, what am I going to do with the rest of my life? What kind of career do I want?"

I thought, "I love photography." Although I didn't have a camera as a child, after Suzanne was born, I learned to use a fully-manual model with a great lens. I took lots and lots of pictures of her as she was growing up. I just loved what the camera did.

I had never done black-and-white photography before, so I decided to take a six-week course at an arts center. My teacher, Rick, was an Ansel Adams type of guy, a no-frills photographer. He became one of my mentors. I took courses from him off and on, and he tutored me one-on-one. Every chance I'd get, I'd try to learn more about photography. I'm such a slow learner that it took me forever for everything to click. I'm not a technical person. I don't think I've ever grasped one true technical concept of photography in my life. I just had this eye for what I wanted to photograph. I had a great feel for it.

Still, people were always telling me, "Don't become a photographer. You won't be able to make a living; it won't be profitable. You should work in the corporate world instead." So I went through a very tormented period about whether or not I should pursue this.

But then I thought, "I have to follow my heart. I have to follow what I feel." One thing I learned from cancer is that you only live once. You have to go for it.

So I enrolled at Brookhaven Community College in Dallas and started taking regular semesters of photography: Photography 1, Photography 2, and so on. All black-and-white. For about three years I took classes part-time, worked part-time at a gift shop and was a full-time mom.

While I was taking these photography courses, the book idea was germinating, formulating. My former sister-in-law, Becky, was very supportive. We've been friends now for thirty years, and she always has the right thing to say to me. She started encouraging me to do the photographs myself. She's the one who put that idea in my head.

Through Becky I met a woman named Dana, and we got to be friends. Then Dana was diagnosed with breast cancer. On a scale of one to ten, it was a ten—very serious. She ended up having a stem-cell transplant, a grueling procedure that's no longer used to treat this type of cancer. The illness brought out the fighter spirit in Dana. She wouldn't let anyone, or anything, knock her down.

I wanted Dana to be photographed in boxing gloves. I knew exactly how I wanted the image to look, but I wanted somebody else to shoot it. I was still so insecure. My issue about photography was always that I was afraid of looking stupid. Even when I was taking classes, I hated getting in a darkroom with a bunch of people. I didn't want them to watch me screw up.

Then I broke my hip. A friend of mine named Lynn who is a commercial photographer heard about my injury and came to see me. I started telling her about my book idea and said that I had this woman named Dana who I wanted to photograph. She said, "Come over and I'll let you use my studio and my medium-format camera. I'll help you set up."

In this woman's studio, I shot my first image: Dana in boxing gloves. Dana didn't have any hair. She had just been through this horrible, horrific experience. She was full of anger, but incredibly strong. That first image was so powerful. I felt like I captured her essence, her soul.

Even more significant than the image itself was the fact that Dana—the very first person I was able to photograph—personified the spirit of my project. The image said, "Look at me. I'm still sexual, I'm still beautiful, I'm still here. I'm a fighter." Creating this image empowered me to make my vision for the book a reality. That was the turning point for me. I was forty-seven years old.

Dana connected me to another woman, and I photographed her. That woman introduced me to two more women, and I photographed both of them. I discovered I was able to capture their essences as well. I was on a roll and started meeting more women to photograph. At this point, though, I only had a handful of images.

If it weren't for Lynn, I wouldn't have gotten started. But after a while I had to stop using her studio and begin to find a way to do this on my own.

Then I met a wonderful portrait photographer. I apprenticed with him for about six months and went with him on shoots. He taught me how to travel with equipment. That's when I bought my medium-format camera, a Mamiya Pro 2. I also bought a portable backdrop and all the equipment I needed to travel. Before this, I had only been shooting locally.

For the project, I was hoping to photograph women from all around the country. So I called the Susan G. Komen Breast Cancer Foundation in Dallas and said to them, "You have a fax newsletter that goes out nationally. I'd like to place an ad in it saying that I'm a photographer looking for breast cancer survivors to photograph."

From running that one ad, I started meeting more and more women outside of Texas. People would call me up and say, "Oh listen, you need to photograph so and so." I collected quite a few images. Each time I photographed a woman, I became more comfortable with the camera, more comfortable with the process and more comfortable with myself.

In response to the ad, I got a call from a woman named Marci in Pittsburgh. She was diagnosed at age twenty-six, and, unfortunately, the cancer had spread to her bones. Like Dana, she was a fighter. I went to photograph her. This was the very first time I got on an airplane with a hundred pounds of equipment and the first time I traveled out of state for the book. Carrying all this luggage by myself and connecting with this stranger and her family gave me such a feeling of accomplishment.

Of course, I had my down moments, one of many being when a woman from Colorado called in response to the ad and took it upon herself to tell me that I should give up on the project. She said I was just wasting my time, that some other woman was also photographing breast cancer survivors and was going to be launching her book at the Komen Race for the Cure that summer.

I went to Becky for solace. She said, "So there's one more book out there. So what? Hers will be last year's book by the time yours is published." Then, in doing some research, I discovered that this woman's project was totally different from what I was doing. I licked my wounds for five minutes and moved on.

On top of this, I went to Santa Fe to photograph three women. When I got there, two of the women called me up and said, "We'd like to see you before you photograph us because we're not real sure about this." We arranged to meet in the restaurant at my hotel. I was thinking to myself, "This is not good." And sure enough, as soon as I sat down, they started drilling me: "Who do you think you are that you can come here and just expect people to pose for you?

What experience do you have? What makes you think you're going to get this book published?" They wanted to know my motives, my family history, and where I ranked in the world. These women were doing their best to humiliate me, telling me I was going to fail. I sat there in total silence. Then finally I came to my senses and said, "You know what? I think we need to end this now."

After they left, I phoned the third woman to confirm our appointment for the next day. She never returned my call. I guess she decided to back out when her two friends backed out. I felt like I was back in high school again.

I spent all that time and money to go to Santa Fe to photograph these women and came home with nothing. I wrote about it in my journal on the plane ride back to Dallas, which was cathartic for me, and felt sorry for myself for about a day. Then I let it go.

What I learned from this experience was to follow the sixth sense I'd been developing as I went around the country meeting women. I knew from my first telephone conversation with the ringleader of these three—before I even got on the plane to Santa Fe—that they weren't right for my project. But I didn't trust my intuition.

Then in 2000, I showed my images to a woman named Barbara on the board of directors for the M.D. Anderson Cancer Center in Houston. She was so moved by what she saw, and she said, "Oh these would be a perfect addition for a fundraiser we're doing at Saks Fifth Avenue in the fall." They used sixteen of my images and, of course, I went to the opening. Hundreds of people were there to buy clothes and support breast cancer research. My images were on the walls of the store and had been blown up to thirty-by-forty feet. They were so powerful-looking, so big and bold. It was exhilarating to see my work for the first time in a large exhibition. As a result of this exposure, there was also an article about me in the *Dallas Morning News*.

In 2001, more great things happened. I'd been wanting to get a magazine to pick up on what I was doing, so I went to New York with my portfolio case. My plan was to pound on some doors and show my images to people. My first night in the city I had dinner with my friend Marlene, who was very supportive of my project and well-connected to the magazine publishing world. She looked at my portfolio and said, "Let me make a few phone calls." Because of her, I got in to see the executive editors of both *Rosie* and *Oprah* magazines.

Rosie and her editors had me photograph women breast cancer survivors nude from the waist up. These images appeared in the October 2001 issue of *Rosie* magazine. Then Oprah used six of my own images for a magazine feature she was doing that same month on cancer among different ethnic groups.

That year I also had an exhibition during Breast Cancer Awareness Month at the Houston Center for Photography, which is one of the finest venues for photography in the United States and is known throughout the world. An old friend of mine named Leslie had introduced me the previous year to the director of the center, which is how I got asked to participate. To walk in and see my name up on the wall of this exhibition space was just incredible. It was truly overwhelming.

After this, the exposure died down, but I still hadn't finished the book. I thought, I'm losing it; the vision is dying. Then I talked to Richard, my nutritionist. I started seeing him after I was diagnosed with breast cancer. He not only helped me heal my body but has also been instrumental in helping me find clarity and strength and direction. "Give it time," he said. "It's not time yet. It will happen." Very powerful words. He believed in me. He kept saying it was going to work out. I needed an outside voice to help me through this process. I owe so much to him, as well as to Becky and my brother Mike. All three have been incredibly supportive.

Anyway, I continued to photograph people, but not as many. I had put so much energy into this project that when I slowed down, I didn't know how I was going to get going again. I was so downtrodden. People started telling me, "You know, Jean, maybe you should put the book aside. Maybe your images aren't meant to be compiled in a book."

On top of this, women were dying. Dana was the first. A few years after her stem-cell transplant, she was re-diagnosed. She fought like a champ again, but finally came to terms with the fact that she was going to die. Before checking herself into a hospice, she called me and said that she wanted my image of her to appear in her obituary. It meant so much to me that she called to tell me this as she was dealing with the finality of her own death.

To this point, three of the women I've photographed have died. A fourth is succumbing to the disease. Every time I meet another woman through this project, I come away thinking how lucky I've been. Compared to some of these women, I had an easier time of it. I also had a family to support me. My mother helped me with my daughter, brought me food and chauffeured me around. Both my parents were there for me, as were my good friends from Houston. There are single women who are diagnosed who don't have that. And because of insurance limitations today, some women now go home the day after their surgery. I've gone through a lot of guilt with this project.

Then in April of 2003, I attended a party and started talking with a friend of mine named Cathy who's connected to the magazine publishing industry. She asked me about the book, and I said, "I don't even want to talk about it. I'm ready to give up." I had been through three literary agents and never even gotten to a publisher. She said matter-of-factly, "Why don't you self-publish?" Because of my connections and hers, it sounded feasible. So she set up an appointment for me with an art director, someone I knew I wanted to use since the beginning of this project. I commissioned him to do a prototype, and he said he would have something for me to look at in a month or so.

Two weeks before the art director and I were scheduled to meet again, Cathy phoned to suggest that I contact Richard Hunt, the publisher of Emmis Books. She said, "Why don't you e-mail him some information about your project and see if he's interested?" So I did. Richard replied not only immediately, but enthusiastically. He told me that his sister was a breast-cancer survivor and that he wanted to bring my project to fruition. The rest is history.

I became a photographer because of breast cancer. Cancer gave me not only the idea for the book, but the strength to do it. My book, though, is about so much more than breast cancer.

Four years into the project, my sister-in-law and I were trying to come up with a title. We decided to call it *Body & Soul: Images of Breast Cancer Survivors*. It was like putting a name to a face. So many women see only their bodies; they don't see their souls. But through the eye of the camera, the lens of the camera, I've been able to capture the souls of the women I've photographed so that the viewers—as well as the subjects themselves—can see what these women are all about. Through my images I'm saying, "Look at these human beings—some of them without hair, some of them without breasts. Look at how beautiful they are. They are still whole." And in the process of doing this book, I have also been able to see my own soul, see my own beauty, see what I am about.

A lot of what I am about is turning a negative into a positive. The book has been a tremendous cathartic experience for me. My relationship with my daughter has also been monumental to this process. She's been my inspiration. I wanted to be the best I could be for her. I wanted to be a role model for her so that she wouldn't fall into the same patterns I had fallen into and make the same mistakes. I wanted her to see me valuing my health and respecting my body. I wanted to create a better life for her, but to do that I had to create a better life for myself. My daughter needed to see me happy.

I'm dealing with relationships differently now, both male and female. And I've learned how to set boundaries and speak up for myself. I've found my voice.

A few years ago, I went to a cancer support group. I said to the women there, "You know, cancer has been a positive thing in my life." One woman got up and said with great anger and frustration in her voice, "Tell me how this is positive. I'm going through chemo for the third time. I don't find anything positive about this." All I could think of to do was to go home and cry. I didn't know how to respond to her. I'm hoping that *Body & Soul* will give women the encouragement and strength that they need.

The book has proved to me that I am strong in my determination. I keep working; I keep pushing; I keep going; I keep finding resources of energy inside of myself, all the while never forgetting to take care of myself mentally, spiritually and physically. When one door closes or someone says, "It can't be done," I'm inspired to work harder. I try not to sell myself short anymore.

I've been thinking recently about all the different events that have contributed to my transformation. It's as if I've had a guardian angel who said to me, "Okay, you're going to wear a brace and you're going to get cancer. Just give it time and you'll see why. You're on a course, you're on a journey, and this journey will bring you to where you want to be. It will help you to know who you really are. And when you get to the end, you'll see how all the dots connect."

When I was planning a trip to London a few years ago, the director of the Houston Center for Photography suggested that I get in touch with a prominent photographer named Simon who lives there. The moment I landed in London I contacted him, and we arranged to meet the very next day for him to critique my work. While viewing the slides of my images, he didn't make a single comment. He was completely silent. But afterwards, he looked up at me and said, "You've arrived, Jean. You're a photographer." ✑

JOURNAL ENTRY 25

A week ago I mailed each of the women I've interviewed her chapter and a release form to sign. I still haven't heard back from two of them. Even though I know better than to wrestle with doubt, all sorts of crazy thoughts have been going through my mind: The women don't like my writing; they feel I haven't captured their voices; they no longer want me to publish their stories. All night I tossed and turned. Then right before I woke up this morning, I had this dream:

I was in the foyer of an old house, walking up a staircase, when I felt something large and furry touch my heel. It was a wolf.

Immediately my heart began racing. I started running up the stairs, but instantly realized that the wolf was faster. Terrified, I decided to levitate. I veered over the banister and ended up in the front hall with my head touching the ceiling and my feet dangling toward the floor.

I thought I was safe, out of the wolf's reach. But no sooner did I have that thought when the wolf mimicked my move. We were now floating face to face, his menacing eyes looking straight into mine.

I didn't flinch. Suddenly I felt no fear. The wolf instantly fell to the ground and dissolved.

After he was gone, I heard the front door open. A tall, thin man with whitish gray hair was standing in the doorway. I thought it was the wolf again, transmuted into human form. I came back down to the ground to face him and for a split second felt my confidence wane.

I looked at him quizzically and said, "Are you the wolf?" He shook his head and replied, "No, you are."

Fear is my enemy. Not terrorism. Not anthrax. Not death. I'm afraid of failure and afraid of success. (How paradoxical!) Almost like magic, though, my wolf dream has left me feeling unafraid.

JOURNAL ENTRY 26

My friend Kathy Krein said to me on the phone the other day, "Don't judge yourself, Prill. So you're dramatic. So you're neurotic. So what!"

JOURNAL ENTRY 27

This past weekend I was driving to Pittsburgh to interview Jane Work, the mother-in-law of my first cousin. I was belting out Joni Mitchell tunes, trying to imitate her high trills and deep, throaty riffs. ("And the sun poured in like butterscotch / and stuck to all my senses.") I love the way she connects with language. Even for a day, I wish I could see the world through Joni Mitchell's eyes.

"IT ISN'T A BAD IDEA TO PAUSE OCCASION-
ALLY FOR AN INWARD LOOK. BY MIDLIFE
MOST OF US ARE ACCOMPLISHED FUGITIVES
FROM OURSELVES."   —John Gardner

JANE WORK
GESTALT THERAPIST

Widowed at age forty-eight, Jane Work entered college during the height of the Vietnam War and went from being a conservative Midwestern housewife to a liberal feminist. She earned a bachelor's degree at age fifty and a doctorate in psychology seven years later. At age sixty-three, after working for various state agencies and school systems, she opened up a private practice. Thirty years after getting licensed, she still sees occasional clients and holds workshops at the retirement home where she now resides.

Irreverent and assertive, she has bright blue eyes and red hair. She's a spitfire and proud of it. Even though she peppers her language with swear words and doesn't suffer fools, inside this spirited octogenarian beats a strong and generous heart.

My first husband died when I was forty-eight. That's really when my life began. Up until then, I didn't know myself very well.

I was raised by my grandparents in New Castle, Pennsylvania. My mother died when I was two, and after that, I only saw my father once in a while. He was a physician in the U.S. Public Health Service.

My grandparents were wonderful and expected me to be a good student. But my grandmother was scared all the time about money. We weren't poor, but she thought we were. So even though I would have liked to have gone to the University of Chicago, my grandmother encouraged me to go to Grove City College—half an hour from New Castle—and get some business skills instead. I did two years of secretarial school. To this day, I still use my shorthand.

When I was eighteen, I began typing at the New Castle Notion Company. Three years later I got a job at American Can, which is how I met my husband, Homer Allen. He had a brother who worked there and introduced us. I stayed at American Can until I got married at twenty-five.

I was in love with my husband. Always. Homer was very generous, but the marriage was difficult. I never really knew what he wanted. He was ten years older than I was and a busy ophthalmologist. Because he had evening office hours and often played cards after work with friends, it seemed like he was never at home.

Homer didn't do much around the house. Men didn't in those days. We had some hired help, but I was very busy doing all the cooking and taking care of our three children. Once I remember hanging twenty-two pairs of little overalls in the basement!

During our marriage, Homer and I constantly socialized with other people. We also entertained his patients and their families in our home. I sometimes think it would have been better to have cut back on all this—to spend more time alone together.

Even when we traveled, friends often came with us. We never took the kids much of anyplace, though, which I thought was sad. One year I took them myself out to a dude ranch in Wyoming. The kids still talk about it—their crowning vacation.

Homer and I were married almost twenty-three years. Toward the end of his life, I think he was working too hard. He was having terrible headaches, and in April of '63 he decided to have some exploratory surgery. It was risky, but being a physician, he didn't want anyone telling him what to do. He had a stroke on the operating table and died ten days later.

It was very traumatic and totally unexpected. Anger has been a great motivator for me, and I was angry with Homer for dying at such a crucial time in our children's lives. My oldest son, Rob, was twenty-one, my daughter, Emily, was nineteen, and my youngest son, Jerry, was eighteen. They just went to pieces. We all did.

The summer after Homer died, three little girls from St. John in the Virgin Islands came to stay with us. Taking them was the best thing I ever did. A good friend of ours named Bill was dating the girls' mother. She wanted to go to the University of Chicago for the summer and work toward getting a degree, but she obviously couldn't do that and take care of her children. I checked it out with my kids, and they said it would be fine if the girls came.

The girls had never been on the mainland of the United States. Lizzie was three, Allison was five and Jacque was six—just about as close together as mine. It was wonderful for all of us. We had a small backyard with a pool, and because Lizzie and Allison were very blond, the chlorine turned their hair green. We called them the little girls with green hair! The continuous commotion kept us all busy. There was no time to mourn.

Off and on over the years, the two younger girls lived with me. I said to Lizzie in an e-mail the other day, "I wish I had adopted you." She wrote back and said, "Well, it's the same as if you had."

That fall I decided to go back to college. I was very tired of being Mrs. Doctor Allen, of being nobody but somebody's wife. I also felt very undereducated. Most of my friends were supportive, but not all. Some thought I should stay home and play bridge. My dear friend Wilbur Flannery, a doctor in New Castle, encouraged me. He became a sort of mentor. He's ninety-six now, and we're still in touch. I wanted to go to school, but I was a little slow in making up my mind. I remember calling him up one day and talking to him about it. He said, "Jane, you have to think ahead."

So at age forty-eight I enrolled at Westminster College in New Wilmington, Pennsylvania, about fifteen minutes from New Castle. Homer had insurance, so fortunately money wasn't a problem. I got credit for the first two years I'd done at Grove City, but that meant I had to stick with business rather than changing my major. I could have stayed at Westminster and gotten a master's in teaching after getting a business degree, but I really didn't want to. You had to go to chapel and there were certain religion courses you had to take. I don't like being told what to do.

Then in the fall of '64, I started dating a man named Paul. He was very nice, very bright, just a wonderful person. He helped to pull me through a lot of the school part and talked me into going to graduate school. It's very hard for anybody to leave New Castle, and by then I'd lived there half a century. Paul helped me—pushed me, really—to move to Cleveland and go to Case Western Reserve. We dated about a year and a half, but then he got sick. He died in 1965. To be honest, that was just one too many losses.

I started graduate school at Case Western Reserve at age fifty. I got a two-bedroom apartment in Cleveland, but I kept the house in New Castle for a couple of years. I came back home on weekends. After I sold the house in '67, my younger son joined me. He took courses in photography and karate and became an expert in ringing for the apartment elevator with his toe.

At this point I hadn't decided to be a therapist, but I knew I wanted to be a doctor of some sort. I started out in audiology, but quickly realized that I could never get a Ph.D. in that field because it involves so much math. I'm not that great in math. So I switched to clinical psychology. It was very difficult, those first few clinical psychology courses. To make matters worse, the head of the department told me he didn't want any housewives in the program. He essentially kicked me out. I was so angry!

I ended up in educational psychology. A guy from Chile was the head of the school psychology students. He was the kind of supervisor that if you were under him, he was dictatorial and awful; but if you were above him, he was just wonderful. Almost all the female students in the school psychology program were my age and had been around. We weren't putting up with his shit. (I have spent many, many hours in group therapy sessions, and my language is pretty colorful at times.)

Overall, though, school was wonderful and the people at Case Western treated me very well. This was the Vietnam era, and Euclid Avenue—the main street running through campus—was filled with protesting students and policemen on horseback. The Kent State killings happened a few miles south. Thank God no one I knew was there.

Dr. Benjamin Spock also taught in my department. I was in one of his big lecture courses. He was gone a lot because he was so famous, and he had a female assistant who took over his classes. Both he and his assistant were very open about sexuality and very anti-war. By this time I was becoming a liberal and a feminist. My world had changed.

Many of my friends were a generation younger. I also became friends with one of my psychology professors. One day we went out to lunch together, and she told me she was going to have everyone in the class write a brief synopsis of their lives. I said that I certainly couldn't do that, and I started to cry. She told me I needed therapy and fixed me up with a renowned Gestalt therapist, Dr. Irving Polster. I was in therapy with him for three years.

The theory of Gestalt is that the sum of the whole is greater than the parts. It is very humanistic and oriented in a present way rather than in the past. That's what I am—a Gestalt therapist. While I was working toward my doctorate, I did a three-year course in Gestalt therapy; and over the years I've taken a great many additional courses at the Gestalt Institute in Cleveland. I enjoyed therapy far more than educational psychology, but I ended up using my school psychology skills in my private practice, too.

During the time I was at Case Western, my foster daughters, Allison and Lizzie, came to live with me in Cleveland for a while. I had a house by then. Lizzie was in third grade and Allie was in fifth, and a girl across the street babysat for them. I was very active and too busy to worry about anything. I was going to school, doing Gestalt work and taking care of the kids.

After I got my master's degree, I spent a year as an intern in the Cleveland public schools. Then I decided to apply for a doctorate. For my dissertation, I worked with a hundred fourth-grade boys selected at random from sixteen Catholic inner-city schools in Cleveland. I enjoyed the case work. At that time, the Catholic schools in Cleveland received no mental health services from the city school system, and they welcomed me.

I finished my doctoral research in 1970. Then it was back to the real world. I left Cleveland and moved with Allison to Evanston, Illinois. (Eventually Allison went to live with her father and his new wife and then entered college and law school. She's married now with two children and is an attorney in Raleigh, North Carolina. She still visits and phones often. We're very close.) I should have stayed in Cleveland to finish my dissertation, but instead I got a job as a psychologist at the Lake County Department of Special Education in Gurnee, Illinois. I worked in a federally-funded program for parents of deaf children.

The program attracted nationally-known speakers. That's how I met Alathena Smith. She was about eighty at the time and an expert on child deafness and on educating parents in dealing with deaf children. She worked at the John Tracy Clinic in California, named after actor Spencer Tracy's deaf son. Alathena was raised in Evanston and came back to give several courses in Gurnee. She always stayed with me. Later, I also visited her in California. I loved her; she was one of my role models and teachers.

During my years in Evanston, I dated a lot. I didn't tell people I was widowed; I pretended I was divorced. Everybody understood "divorced." I also did photography—I love doing black-and-white—and had a darkroom for many, many years. It's fun. You know, a darkroom is a wonderful place to have a date.

Around this time, I met a woman in Evanston who was the religious education director of the First Unitarian Church. She was about my age. Her name was Bea. We started a singles' group with about six other people and met at each other's houses until the group got too big. Then we started meeting in the church. People came from miles around. We always met on Sunday nights because that was when the divorced fathers had to take the kids back to their mothers. The men brought the wine and the women brought the snacks. It was very successful. We had no speeches, just music and dancing. I've had so many losses throughout the years, and I've discovered two ways to get out of a depression. One is to do some creative writing; another is to dance. The point of the group was not to get married or get a date. It was not a hook-up kind of thing. The point was just to have fun.

Then in 1972 I got a letter from Case Western saying that if I didn't write up my dissertation, I wouldn't get my doctoral degree. A friend of mine said, "Jane, the magic word is O-U-T." I had more credit hours than anyone ever needed.

When I told my friend Richard about the letter, he said, "Come down to my apartment, stay here, bring your typewriter and WRITE IT!" Another wonderful man, Ray, helped me with the statistical analysis. I received my Ph.D. in 1973. I was finally a doctor—not a doctor's wife or a doctor's daughter, but a doctor in my own right.

After I got my doctorate, I quit my special education job and commuted thirty miles to Wisconsin, working as a school psychologist in five different schools. I did this for two years. Then one of my sons suggested I answer an ad for a job as the director of psychology at the Marion Area Counseling Center in Marion, Ohio. I applied and got it. By then I was about sixty.

I lived in Marion for two years. People will say to me, "Oh, did you know so and so from Marion, Ohio?" And I say to them, "If they weren't mentally disturbed, I did not know them." It's true. I also did some radio programs and was on a telephone help line. I worked very hard.

While I was in Marion, Lizzie came to live with me again at my house in the country. She was a high school senior. All the other students had known each other since kindergarten. The poor girl! It was terrible. That's when we got Shakespeare, our Springer Spaniel. That winter it snowed. And snowed. The following spring Lizzie graduated and went off to Lewis & Clark College in Portland, Oregon. She's now a professor at the University of Alaska in Dillingham.

Two years after I moved to Marion, I fell in love with Bill Work. I'd been single for fifteen years. He was a tall man with a pleasant smile. Both men and women liked him. Without any encouragement from him, I think he could have had any woman he wanted.

Bill's cousin Elizabeth had married my uncle many years ago, so I had known Bill before this. But I didn't know him well, and he was married. When his wife died, though, I invited him to come to Marion. He declined. He thought I wanted to fix him up with some other woman! We both had power of attorney for my Aunt Elizabeth; so when she became ill, we began consulting on the phone a lot. After Aunt Elizabeth died, we met in Florida to help settle her estate.

Right away we knew we were meant for each other. We liked each other immediately. We went out for a chocolate sundae, and

I think that was the end. My son Jerry said, "You're going to marry him." And I did. We married a few months after we met in Florida, on January 1, 1979. My name is now Jane McKinney Allen Allen Work. I was born an Allen and married an Allen. (I put the McKinney in after I went to live with my grandparents.)

After Bill and I got married, we bought a house in Mount Lebanon, Pennsylvania, near Pittsburgh. At first, he was still getting over his wife's death. She'd only been dead about nine months. He'd talk about her, and that bothered me. But just last year I said to him, "You know, we've reached the place where we can talk about our first marriages without either of us getting upset. And that's a pleasant place to be."

We had such a good relationship. I finally realized, though, that two things would never change about Bill. First, he would always be a Presbyterian. The Dalai Lama came here, and I didn't get to see him. I was so mad! Second, he would always be a Republican.

Jerry says we got along by negotiating. Once Bill and I were going to vote for different people in a local election. We put campaign placards for the two of them in our front yard with "his" and "hers" signs over each. A picture of this was in the local press.

In our prior marriages, we had both been with other couples when we traveled. We decided this time around to travel by ourselves. We went to China, Europe and all across the States.

After I married Bill, I wanted to go into private practice right away; but first I had to pass a test to get licensed in Pennsylvania. I got up the morning of the test and said to Bill, "What am I going to do if I fail?"

He said, "Well, you'll just be my wife."

I said, "Oh shit."

I passed, barely. I am not good at those "pick-the-best-choice-out-of-four" tests. I opened a practice in a small office in Mt. Lebanon. My practice was almost entirely with single women and small children. I know an awful lot about being single, and I feel like I've lived enough to be helpful. I've been through just about everything.

I'm also a sex therapist. At my age, women are so afraid of having a physical relationship. The men are even more afraid than the women. It's so funny. But as a psychologist, I know how important it is for older people to have a close, physical relationship— not necessarily sex, but physical contact.

Then, in 1994, I became quite ill with congestive heart failure. I was in the hospital for five weeks and not expected to live. But after my heart stopped and the doctors used the paddles on me, my heart returned to normal and I finally went home. I'm sure that much of my recovery was due to the hundreds of prayers said by my children, their friends and my own friends. Bill pushed me around in a wheelchair, even taking me to the National Gallery in Washington, D.C. He said he liked going slowly through the art gallery and being able to sit down often!

After I got better, we decided to move here to Friendship Village, which is a retirement facility. It's very segregated, the men and the women. A few couples "go steady," but no one actually shacks up. Against the rules, I guess. Oh well. . .

I've given several workshops here using Herbert Benson's "Relaxation Response," which is a form of meditation. I use soft music and aromatic candles and quietly give instructions on relaxation. Learning to completely relax one's body seems to help prevent all kinds of stress-related illnesses.

I'm still licensed. It's really important for me to keep licensed and stay a psychologist. It took too much to get here. I have to complete thirty continuing education hours by November 30th. I attended a boring workshop last week—all about writing psychological reports—that almost fulfilled my requirement.

I've told many of my clients, "Even if you just take basket

weaving, go back to school." Many did. School sure changes one's mind about all sorts of fixed ideas. I tell people that they won't necessarily know any more when they have a Ph.D., but people will think they do.

I've been a licensed psychologist for thirty years and practiced on my own about twenty. I think I did very well with most of my clients. I've enjoyed it tremendously. I helped one young woman up until a few months ago.

So here I am, married twice, widowed twice and retired. My beloved Bill died a few months ago after a yearlong illness. We were married twenty-four years, longer than I was married the first time.

My children, foster children and stepchildren have mostly married and had children of their own. All of them are very caring, and I feel very fortunate.

Recently, an old boyfriend in Lewisville, Texas, said he'd like to come up and see me, but these days he's only able to drive to Wal-Mart and is too scared to fly. He's only eighty-nine. What a chicken!

As you get older and more besieged with friends dying, it seems that one mourns a few days, takes a deep breath and walks slowly ahead. I'm eighty-seven years old now, and that involves a lot of living. I don't want to sound like I was a big angel, because I certainly wasn't. But I've enjoyed my life. ✒

JOURNAL ENTRY 28

Yesterday I gave my mom the first nine chapters to read. I was anxious to learn how she'd react to the journal entries that describe my feelings toward my father. In spite of his flaws, she loved him deeply. I didn't want to upset her.

She phoned early this morning. As always, she was incredibly supportive. But this experience has given me a greater appreciation for what I'm asking people to do when I give them a release to sign. Even though this book is a quick read, I don't want anyone to gloss over the tremendous courage it's taken for some of these women to go public with their stories.

JOURNAL ENTRY 29

Song I made up in the shower this morning:

All around me I see angels
They are walking down the street
They are in the supermarket
They are dancing on two feet.

JOURNAL ENTRY 30

In the fall of 2001, I placed a short advertisement in the International Women's Writing Guild newsletter seeking late bloomers. Over a hundred women replied. A Detroit writer named Elizabeth Buzzelli was one of them.

Elizabeth told me that her good friend Rainelle Burton was the most unusual woman she'd ever met and that she had an amazing tale of late blooming. In April of 2002, I flew to Michigan to interview them both. (I originally planned to include the women as a pair—each has a wonderful story to tell—but ultimately decided to limit the book to one writer.)

The day I arrived, Rainelle had a medical emergency and ended up in the hospital. Last August, I tried to interview her again, this time at a writer's conference in Saratoga Springs. At the last minute, she decided not to attend. Then in April of 2003, I flew back to Detroit, determined finally to meet her.

The timing was perfect; her story was well worth the wait.

"TRUST IN YOURSELF. YOUR PERCEPTIONS ARE OFTEN FAR MORE ACCURATE THAN YOU ARE WILLING TO BELIEVE."   —Claudia Black

RAINELLE BURTON
WRITER

Held a virtual prisoner by her family until she was eighteen, Rainelle Burton grew into adulthood with little knowledge of how to get along in the world. Dealing with dyslexia, homelessness and depression, she raised two boys and worked at Michigan Blue Cross for more than twenty years. At the age of fifty-two she published a critically-acclaimed first novel, *The Root Worker,* which was selected as a Borders Books Recommended Book and a Great Lakes Book Award finalist. She's currently a writer-in-residence at Wayne State University and is working on a second novel.

Dark-skinned and gap-toothed, she's irrepressibly, unabashedly herself and one of the most beautiful beings I've ever met. Although she's been through hell, she's emerged from the experience without a trace of soot on her spirit.

Here I am. This is me! It took years and years for me to really become me. I was in my forties. Ain't that something?

I grew up an outsider, like the character Ellen in my book *The Root Worker.* My life was not *The Root Worker.* That didn't happen to me, okay? But, like Ellen, I didn't fit in. I didn't fit in with my family. I didn't fit in with my community. I didn't fit in with my peers.

My world was a little-bitty box. I couldn't go anywhere because my mother wouldn't allow it. I went to school and came home. Period. It was clear to me from the beginning—so clear—

that I couldn't go outside. My four brothers and sister could, but I couldn't. I didn't even ask. It was understood.

This all started when I was very little. And because it was so much a part of the way things were, it didn't seem odd to me. Even though it was a hard thing to go through, it didn't feel hard.

I realize now that I couldn't allow myself to feel. Otherwise I would have been so incredibly lonely and so incredibly hurt that it would have been too much. I wouldn't have been able to bear it. So I was unaffected by what was happening on one level, but I was affected. It's taken me this many years to even say it was hard. I still don't feel the hugeness of the isolation—but then my mother isolated all of her children from each other.

So the beginning of my story has to be about my mother and what is not known about her mother. There was a huge silence there. I don't know what it could have been about my grandmother that made all nine of her children never once mention her after they grew up and left home. It must've been something horrible.

The only description my mother ever gave me of my grandmother turned out to be a lie. She said her mother had light brown skin and long hair all the way down her back. Years later I saw a picture, and it showed a dark-skinned woman with short hair. She looked like me. When I saw that picture, I knew it had everything to do with my relationship with my mother.

My mother's people were West Virginia people. Her father was a coal miner, and they were dirt poor. In a coal mining town, you don't own anything. You live in a mining shack and you owe your soul to the company store. You don't do anything in a proper way; you do everything in a useful way. Whatever works—that's what you do. And in this culture of resourcefulness, kids are not always treasured and loved. They're there to help you survive. There's not much room for anything else.

My father's people, on the other hand, were Georgia people.

They believed in education, and my father's sisters were all teachers. In the South the proper way of doing things is very important. So your image is important and the way you look is important and how you do things is important, especially if you're trying to make your way in a white world.

So there was this huge culture clash between my parents. What seemed practical in my father's world—always being proper—seemed so unnecessary in my mother's world. In my father's family, a lamp was for light and had to be displayed a certain way. In my mother's family, a lamp could be a coat rack if you needed one.

When my mother married my father, he and his brother owned a store with a four-family flat above it. But by the time my twin brother, Raymond, and I came along, the store had folded, my father was out of work, and the six of us were living in one of the four apartments. This was in Black Bottom, on the lower-east side of Detroit. The lower down you went, the more poverty-stricken it was. Black Bottom was the bottom of the low.

Growing up, I was like the lamp. I was there to be used. If I was in the kitchen washing dishes and someone wanted me to go to the other room and turn on the television set, that's what I had to do.

One time, my older brother, who's dead now, made some coffee and poured it in a glass. Of course, the glass broke. You can't put hot coffee in a glass! I was upstairs and didn't know what had happened. When my mother came home and saw the mess, she had a fit. My brother told her the truth, but she didn't get angry at him. She got angry at me. She said, "Rainelle, get your ass down here!" I told her I didn't even know about the glass, and she said, "Well you should have known. You should have come down here to check." She beat the hell out of me. I really thought I had done something wrong.

The year I turned eight, my mother and father had an argument about me. My father wanted to get us all something for Christmas, but my mother said, "Well there's just not enough money to go around. Rainelle will understand." Then she turned to me and said, "Won't you, Rainelle?"

I said, "Yeah, I'll understand."

But I didn't understand, because I came downstairs the next day and everyone had something but me. My brothers got bikes. My sister got a doll. And I didn't get anything. Nothing. I mean zero. And that was painful. That hurt. But then it got to be what I expected. I didn't expect to get Christmas presents.

Home was horrible, but I loved school. My twin brother, Raymond, and I went to school together my whole life. For twelve years we were stuck together like glue.

I was dyslexic, so I couldn't read. All the letters looked like a series of zeroes and ones. Dyslexia changes as you get older, but this was what I saw in the beginning.

The good thing was that Raymond and I were always in the same class. He would read the words to me, and I would make sense of them. Together we made one reader. I was good at the comprehension thing. I'd tell him what everything meant. That's how we did our homework.

I also really paid attention in class because it was so important to me that no one find out I couldn't read. I listened carefully to how words sounded together. I trained myself. I could almost ad lib what was going to come next.

Then when I was about eleven, the words started taking some shape. The letters were backward, but now I could interpret them. Writing was still a problem, though. I'd write backward on the board. My teachers thought I knew better. They thought I was acting up, and they'd make me go stand out in the hall. But what I was writing looked exactly the way everything they were writing looked to me. I couldn't see a difference. None. If you put the two side by side, they looked the same to me. I couldn't even imagine what was wrong.

Finally, when I was about twelve, the reading/writing thing just took off. It was so amazing. Wow! I was going around reading everything. When it clicked, boy did it click! I had found the missing piece and now I could see the whole picture.

Even to this day, though, I can't look in a mirror and put on makeup or comb my hair. My hands are going all over the place. I can't transfer what I'm doing to the image I'm seeing in the mirror. And if I don't go the same way every day when I'm driving, I still get turned around. When you grow up with dyslexia, you really do have the sense that nothing is what it seems.

Anyway, the reading thing was great. But when I turned fourteen my mother decided to take me out of school. She thought I was old enough to get a job. It's back to the lamp thing. My twin brother had a fit. He said, "If you don't let Rainelle go to school, I'm going to run away from home." He meant it, and she knew he meant it. My mother loved my twin brother; she adored him. So even though she didn't like it, she let me continue going to school. I went because of Raymond. We were still helping each other—the twins.

I graduated at eighteen and set out to find a job. From our house, you could see the outline of downtown Detroit. It was kind of pulling at me, that outline. So I just walked toward it.

Every day I walked downtown and went into different buildings, to different companies, and applied for jobs. But I was this huge oddball. I wasn't really dressed right. And there's a weirdness about you when you're not used to being around people, when you've been that isolated.

People started giving me advice: "Honey, if you want a job, you'll have to dress better than that." Still, it was like a Catch-22, because how are you going to dress better if that's all you own and you don't have a job?

The post office finally hired me to sort mail. For a couple of weeks, I walked to work and walked back. It was about an hour and a half each way. But after I got my first paycheck, I thought I'd try to catch the bus. Then it dawned on me: I didn't know how to catch the bus. Here were all these buses going everywhere. How did you know which one to take?

I just stood where a lot of people were and caught the first one that came along. But when I stepped up onto the bus, the driver looked at me and said, "Aren't you going to put the money in?"

"How much is it?" I asked. "Where do I put it?"

The bus driver thought I was crazy. He said, "Where are you from?" He couldn't believe I was from Detroit and had never gotten on a bus. I didn't even know that to get off, you had to ring the bell. That first time I rode all the way to the end of the line.

So that was really a learning experience. It took me about seven or eight times before I finally got it. Nothing made sense to me. But, like the reading thing, when I got it, I just took off. I was catching buses everywhere!

After I'd been at the post office for a while, a co-worker of mine asked me to go to the show—you know, to the movies. It was incredible. I'd never been to the show before. I'd never been on a date! So I went out and bought this formal, pink strapless gown and satin shoes. But when I got to the show, I saw that nobody but me was dressed up. Everyone was looking at me like I was nuts. It was awful. Horrible, horrible.

The post office job lasted about a year. Then I applied to Michigan Blue Cross. I was nineteen. The woman there said she'd call me when there was an opening. I knew what that meant, that she wasn't ever going to call. So the next day I phoned her back and said, "I haven't heard from you yet, so I'm calling to check."

She said, "You were just here yesterday. You must need a job really bad."

I said, "I do."

So she said, "Well, come on down and we'll see where we can fit you in." I was hired as a clerk and started at Blue Cross in '69. I worked there twenty-three years.

It was great at Blue Cross, but I was always in trouble. I'd get in trouble just for being me. More than once, I came to work with my clothes on inside out. So here I was, this odd person.

Everyone was always trying to change me for my own good. It was like, "She'd be a good person if she were normal." They said I didn't take the job seriously. And they were right. I didn't take the job seriously. I didn't worry about things. If the bus got stopped by a train and I was late for work, then okay, so I was late for work. They'd say, "Well, we're going to have to write you up." And it would be, like, okay, write me up. Then they'd be upset because I wouldn't be upset about that. Well, there was nothing to be upset about. They'd tell me I could lose my job, and I'd say, "That's okay. If you have to fire me, then fire me." But I turned out to be such a good worker that they kept me on.

Then when I was twenty-one, I met my ex-husband. He worked at Blue Cross as a garage attendant. I knew I wasn't in love with him, but I loved that he liked me. I had no dating experience, except for that one time I went to the show. He ended up moving in with me. A couple of years later I got pregnant with my son Tiran.

My ex-husband and I had a really dysfunctional relationship. When my son was about three months old, my husband started keeping the money I gave him to pay the rent. So one day after picking up Tiran from day care, I came home and found all our things out on the street. We'd been evicted.

Then I remembered that I still had a car. I don't remember what kind of car it was or what color. All I remember is that I was so happy to see that car parked a few blocks away. Tiran and I lived in that car for three months.

It was February, and it was cold outside. So I'd run the car to keep warm, and I'd wake up at different intervals during the night to turn it back on for a while. I also learned where all the gas stations were that had bathrooms with running water and paper towels. I'd warm Tiran's formula in a gas station sink, then wash up and go to work. I took my two outfits that I had salvaged to a laundromat. All my other clothes had been put out on the street.

I didn't let anyone at work know I was homeless. I didn't even think we were homeless. I just knew that we didn't have an apartment to live in. I mean it felt so normal, even though I knew it wasn't. But I realized that if anyone found out I was living in a car, the baby would be taken away from me. So I never parked it in the same place twice.

A few years ago a friend and I were watching television, and I saw this homeless family living in a van. I felt so terrible for them. I thought, "Oh my God, they're homeless with those kids and everything." And then it dawned on me: I had been homeless! I said to my friend that I wasn't homeless like that. But I was homeless like that—only I had a car, not a van.

Still, it wasn't the end of the world. Yeah, a house would have been a heck of a lot better than a car. But I think when you go through this kind of thing, it gives you a different perspective on what's earth-shattering and horrible and what's not. And on that scale, it wasn't all that big.

Anyway, after three months I'd saved up enough money to put down a security deposit on another apartment. And then, wouldn't you know, my husband reappeared. I finally left him for good when Tiran was three. I wasn't angry when I left. There was just a realization that I couldn't live with him for the rest of my life. I knew it would destroy us.

When I left my husband, I got a job as a live-in baby-sitter. I still worked at Blue Cross during the day, but I baby-sat at night. After a year or so, I was able to save enough to buy a small house, a colonial, on the west side of Detroit. I was twenty-seven. I'd really arrived!

By this time Blue Cross was becoming computerized. They were offering free computer programming classes, but my supervisor wouldn't let me take one. She didn't think I had the aptitude. The truth is, she didn't know anything about me. Then I got my hands on one of the workbooks. It was like I knew exactly what this computer thing was. It was just like the zeroes and ones from my childhood. I didn't even have to finish reading the workbook.

To make a long story short, I said to my supervisor, "I know this stuff. I can do it. Just give me a chance." She didn't want to, but the manager said to her, "Let Rainelle try." So they gave me all these problems to do. They were so easy. I knew how the computer functioned. I could visually see it in my head. I started solving all these problems for everyone. They were really amazed. I ended up being a systems expert.

The problem is that I'd been hired as a clerk. I couldn't get a raise or a promotion. I couldn't get anything. Here I was this clerk doing all this systems stuff. I did this for ten or twelve years. Then I got mad as hell. I couldn't take it anymore. So I decided to quit.

I wrote a little memo giving my two-weeks' notice—just a couple of lines saying I was leaving. But when my supervisor read it, she said, "You can't quit. Where are you going to go? You don't know anything other than this." And I thought, you know what? She's right. This has been my whole life. She didn't mean it that way, but I did.

So I didn't quit and I didn't get a raise. All that happened from writing that memo was that I had a huge revelation. And that was enough.

That's when I decided to go to back to school. I enrolled at Wayne State University. I took classes at night after work and on the weekends. I went nuts. Once I got into it, I was really into it.

I didn't even want another job; I just wanted to learn. I was majoring in interdisciplinary studies.

But right before it was time to do my senior essay, I got pregnant with my son Raymond. I was thirty-five, and Tiran was twelve. I was bedridden—really, really sick. I was one essay away from getting my degree, but never got it. After my book was published, though, Wayne State hired me to teach some classes. Right now I'm teaching a course called "Creative Writing in the Social Sciences."

Anyway, at the time I got pregnant I was living with Raymond's father. He was a nice guy. Really sweet. But then he disappeared. One day he didn't show up at work. I don't know if he died or what. Raymond was almost two years old when it happened. It was horrible at first not to know, but now it's okay. Maybe that's my own denial. I'd rather not think that something that drastic happened to him. I'd rather think he just had a change of heart. I never heard from him again. He disappeared off the face of the earth.

After moving here to Belleville, I decided I didn't want another man; and boy did I start having a good time just living. I didn't turn against men. I love men, and I have a lot of male friends. But when I stopped dating men and just started being friends with them, it was wonderful. I mean they're so much fun. I think they're incredible—just not for me to be in a relationship with.

Anyway, I moved here thirteen years ago. I left my house in Detroit because the neighborhood started changing when Tiran was a teenager. There was a real problem with drugs and gang warfare. I knew all the neighborhood kids from the time they were small and had pulled some of them out of crack houses in the middle of the night while my own kids were home sleeping. I was trying to save them, but there was no saving to be done. That was hard.

After a couple of years of this, some kids ended up getting

killed. Each one of them had this look in his eyes like he knew he was next. Every one of them knew. One day I came home from work and Tiran had that look.

That was the worst thing that I've ever been through in my whole life. I mean nothing was worse than that. Oh God! I saw that look, and I knew what that was. I knew I didn't have time to think about what I needed to do. I just put my kids in the car and got on the freeway and drove. Tiran was sixteen. I had to get him away from there because I knew he was going to die if I didn't. Period. I didn't know when—what time or what day. But I knew I was running for his life.

I ended up here. I'd never been to this town before; I'd never even heard of Belleville. I just wanted to get far enough away so that my son wouldn't be their next victim—whoever they were. I saw these apartments from the freeway and stopped to ask about them. The manager said she had one for rent, and I said to her, "I'll take it right now. Today."

I left everything behind and moved my kids in here. The next day I met with a real estate lady to arrange to put my house up for sale. But the house had been shot up. Completely shot out. Either that morning or the night before, they'd come. The real estate lady said, "Well, we can't put the house up for sale like this." And I said, "I'll figure out something." Then I came back here and never went back. I never did sell the house. I just let it go.

If Tiran had known we were leaving for good, he might not have wanted to come. But as it was, he took it in stride. One of his new friends said to me a while after we moved in, "Tiran told me you saved his life." And I said, "I know." So Tiran knew, and he knew that I knew.

I'm getting ready to buy a condo. It took me this many years to trust myself to buy another place. All this time I didn't want to own anything again because I wanted to be free to leave if I had to. It's taken me this long to realize it's okay. I don't have to run from anything anymore.

After we'd been there about six months, Blue Cross got a brand-new computer system. By that time, I was a corporate trainer and systems analyst, and I was hand-picked as a part of a team of experts to get the new system up and running. You need to know about every little detail, because if just one little thing is off, the whole thing doesn't work. So I was asked to write the systems manuals. That's when Blue Cross promoted me to technical writer.

Life was great. I had this place. I had my kids. I was making pretty good money. And then I fell apart. I mean I literally went nuts. I was hospitalized nine times in two years.

During this time, Tiran took care of Raymond. He took care of us all. That was a side of him I didn't know before. Then after the second breakdown, Blue Cross wouldn't let me come back.

I was there, but I wasn't present. I couldn't do anything. I couldn't respond to anything. I wasn't even interacting with my kids. Everything was like a fog.

After six or seven months with no change, I sort of thought, "This is how my life is going to be from now on." At first I was sad. I was so used to being able to do everything. But then when I reconciled myself to the idea that I would probably never be able to do anything again and there was nothing that could be done about it, I wasn't sad anymore. Just flat.

The sadness is mourning your inability to do things. You only feel sad when you put yourself in the past or the future: I wish I were this, or I wish I could do that. But if you're not fighting it, depression itself is flat. And in this flatness, you are outside of your own existence. You're in this gray place where you can't feel anything. You can't respond. It's like watching a movie where you can see and hear things the characters who are interacting don't see and hear. They're concerned about their lines and how they're going to respond and what they're going to say, but you aren't.

I was on Prozac. It didn't help or hurt. It did nothing at all. I found out later that my twin brother was hospitalized for depression at the same time. That's how parallel our lives were at that point.

Then after two years, it lifted. One day I woke up and it was gone. All of a sudden, everything was so clear. I mean everything. I had never been that clear. It was almost too clear, too brightly clear. It was like I knew everything that everybody was going to say to each other, every way that everyone was going to respond. It all seemed so obvious. My friends nicknamed me "The Buddha." The next time I got depressed, I welcomed it. I was happy for the flatness so I'd be clear again.

I was also able to finally finish *The Root Worker*. I had started it three or four years earlier. Everything I'd been struggling with suddenly seemed so easy. I just went through and rewrote the whole thing. It took no time at all. When you're clear, you can move mountains. When you're crystal clear, mountains aren't even mountains anymore!

The whole thing about the book is that I'd never seriously thought about writing before. When I was a kid, I wanted to be a writer. That was a dream I had. I wrote poetry and I thought I was going to be the next Robert Burns. But when I grew up, I had to make a living.

My friend Peter gave me the idea. He was telling me I should read *Midnight in the Garden of Good and Evil,* and we started talking about voodoo. Root working is a derivative of voodoo. It comes from West Africa. (I explained all this in the reader's guide I did for the Penguin edition.) Anyway, Peter started asking me about root workers, and I was trying to tell him what root working does to people—the whole mistrust and manipulation that goes along with it. I told him that the way it's presented in popular literature wasn't accurate. And he said, "You know, you really need to write a book about all this."

I started out do to a little nonfiction piece. But it didn't make sense because there's no way that you can explain that world—language distorts the sense of what it really is. So I wondered if there was any way I could put someone right in that world to see what root working is. And I decided that's what I wanted to do. That was my original vision. And then it really hit me that this is what fiction is.

As I said, the things in the book didn't happen to me. That wasn't my life. But I grew up in a community where root working took place. It was a given in that world. And being an outsider, you see all of that.

I wanted to separate myself from what I thought and felt about it. To write the book, I had to find out what this root working thing really was outside of what happens in it. That's how the character, Ellen, came about. Who else could talk about it without putting some kind of morality to it? Who could be there without making judgments? A child. So when Ellen appeared, it was cool. Root working was so much a part of her, so much a part of what she had to endure.

The basic story was written the first year. But I knew the story had to be more than just what happened. I went on this journey to find out what I didn't know—what made the people in this world like this. That's when everything started taking shape. That's when the character Barbara came in. She's the light of the story. I had to go through my own journey before there could even be a Barbara.

I had to do huge work on myself. Not therapy. Just me by myself. Before the depression, there was this big "What?" I had all the why's, but none of the answers. Looking back, I realize now I was on a path to find myself. The depression separated me from what I thought I knew, and in that separation were the answers.

After the depression lifted, I picked up the book and saw all these layers and layers of isolation. It was so incredible. I wrote a whole new draft that wove that thread of isolation through the whole story. I was able to connect all the little dots so that the truth was there.

Then I had to find an agent. I'd actually found a publisher before the depression. But two years later when I came out of it, the woman was no longer around. I thought, "Well, I'll just have to start all over again." By that time, though, I was pretty savvy. I'd gone to writer's conferences and talked to editors and agents and all that. I knew what to do. I got an agent at James Levine Communications who sold my book to Overlook. Everything worked out fine. I was fifty-two when it was published in 2001. Then Penguin turned around and bought the paperback rights.

My publicist at Overlook—he's with Miramax now—was great. I found out that the book was going to be featured in Oprah's magazine in June of 2001. I went crazy! I called the agency and said, "I know James Levine is busy, but I thought he needed to know that my book is coming out in *Oprah* and that Oprah's people are going to be considering it for her book club." It wasn't even five minutes later when James Levine called me back.

He said, "Hello, Rainelle. This is Jim. I've been meaning to call you. I wanted to invite you to a party I'm having."

He said Jim, not James!

I said, "I'll be there."

I thought this party would be sometime down the road. But when I got the e-mail, it said the party was that coming Saturday and that it was a masquerade ball. The party was by invitation only, but I called some friends and asked them if they wanted to come with me. I got a ninety-nine dollar round-trip fare. It was like flying on a crop-duster. The plane shook all the way!

When we got there, Jim came to the door. He said, "Oh Rainelle, so glad to see you." Then he said, "Are these people with you?"

I said, "Yeah. That's okay, ain't it?"

He said, "Oh yes. Come on in." There were all these chi-chi people, and here we were looking like us. We weren't even wearing masks!

Then the doorbell rang. It was my friend Hannelore from the International Women's Writing Guild and her daughter Elizabeth Julia. They came with this woman from Georgia who was as big as I am. She looked like she was going to break into a gospel song. Hannelore said to Jim, "Rainelle invited us."

Then all of a sudden it got real quiet, and I heard a voice say, "Rainelle." It was my publicist. He was so sexy—all in black. He had black jeans and a black leather jacket with a white, white shirt. Sleeves rolled up. Chest open. Hair tousled just enough. He was leaning against a wall. He looked like he had just stepped out of Hollywood. Movie-star gorgeous. Oh man, when I saw him, I said, "Who can say no to you?" He was only thirty years old. Everyone was asking, "Who is that man?"

My publicist apologized for being late. He said he'd been on the phone with a production company that was interested in the film rights to my book. The next thing I knew, those words were reverberating throughout the room: "Film rights, film rights."

Then he said that Oprah was reading my book as a possible book club selection and that Penguin wanted to buy the paperback rights. Then I heard, "Oprah, Oprah." Wow! It was crazy.

The next day I went to meet with Jim to talk about the publicity plan for the book. My publicist sent a car to pick me up. But after I left the agency, I got really sad. It just hit me that my life wouldn't be the same anymore. I cried and cried. My friend Elizabeth thought Jim had said something really nasty to me. But I told her, "No. He was great. He said all good things."

"Well, then, what's wrong with you?" she asked.

And I said, "I love my life. I don't want my life to change."

The good news is that nothing really changed. As you can see, I'm still living in the same place. The book was in the magazine. I heard that Oprah read it, but she stopped doing her book club two months before the book came out in paperback. In terms of the film rights, it's still open. So that's exciting, too. Just because it gets picked up, though, doesn't mean it's going to be a film. Whatever happens, happens. I'm working on a new book now.

It's all about trust. Because when you trust, life just takes off and becomes something you couldn't even imagine it was going to be. You don't need to plan it all out. Like I said, whatever is supposed to happen, will happen." People say, "Well, what if it doesn't?" But that's okay, too. You'll still get up in the morning and breathe. I just can't wait to get out of bed each day to be me. ✑

People keep asking what I've learned writing this book, but encapsulating my thoughts without trivializing my experience is proving to be quite a difficult task. So much of what I've been taught these last three years can't be stuffed into sound bites. That said, here are some of my observations:

1. Getting started is the hard part: Inertia works positively and negatively. When you're stuck in your life, it takes a lot of effort to get unstuck. (It took me more than a year to work up the courage to begin writing the first story.) But once you make the effort and start going in a new direction, it's relatively easy to keep on going.

2. The importance of persistence can't be overstated. All the women I interviewed experienced setbacks and lost their momentum, but they didn't allow themselves to wallow in self-pity. They might have wanted to give up, but they kept right on going.

3. It's critical to focus on the goal rather than the obstacles. These women didn't say, "I'll never get hired because of age discrimination," or "I can't do this because I don't have enough money." Like a ballerina who looks at a spot in the distance as she pirouettes across the stage, they kept their eyes fixed on their dreams.

4. Nothing you like to do is tiresome: From the outside looking in, it sounds daunting to go to medical school at forty-six, join the Peace Corps at sixty-five, become a

flight attendant at seventy-one. But the truth is that it isn't exhausting; it's exhilarating. It's far more tiring to do something you don't enjoy.

5. A sense of humor helps. Most of the women in this book love to laugh—especially at themselves!

6. Listening to their hearts turned out to be, in the long run, the most unselfish thing these women had ever done. They might not have made dinner for their families every night, but they inspired their children and the people around them. Without exception, they are now using their talents to help others. In the process of blossoming, in other words, these women have connected more powerfully than ever before with the human community.

JOURNAL ENTRY 32

Even though Rainelle Burton's story turned out to be the most significant for me, I'm putting Wini's story last. Because she was my inspiration for writing, and because her example launched my personal journey of self-discovery, it seems fitting that I end with her. In doing so, I bring this book full circle and honor the importance of role models, which from the beginning has been both the power and the purpose of this project.

"THE WORLD IS ROUND AND THE PLACE
WHICH MAY SEEM LIKE THE END MAY ALSO
BE ONLY THE BEGINNING."
                    —Ivy Baker Priest, Former U.S. Treasurer

WINI YUNKER

Born and raised in the small town of Nicholasville, Kentucky, Wini Yunker was devastated when the Peace Corps rejected her at age twenty-six. She waited almost four decades before reapplying. During the intervening years, she raised a son, rose through the ranks at the Sargent & Greenleaf lock company, and studied nights and weekends to complete her education. At age sixty-five, she finally fulfilled her dream and left the States for a two-year tour in Ukraine.

Wearing her trademark long, dangling earrings (yellow ones to match her yellow outfit), she's short and plump, with a warm smile and a cap of silver hair. Despite her grandmotherly appearance, she's surprisingly athletic. She caves and climbs and, at the age of fifty-eight, even learned to ski. No longer young in years, she's still a kid at heart.

When I was growing up, it was really isolated, really provincial here in Nicholasville. I dreamed of traveling. To this day, my son Joe and I always keep our suitcases packed!

World War II started when I was seven. I had these five big sisters, and both my sister Zenie's husband and my sister Sarah's husband went to the South Pacific. So I heard about being overseas from them. The first time I left Kentucky, though, was in my teens when we went to Cincinnati. They had tall buildings there—gosh, like thirty-five stories.

As a kid, I didn't talk much. My sisters did all the talking. But I was adventuresome. When I was twelve, I climbed to the top of the courthouse cupola. Then I doubled up on some courses and skipped my junior year of high school, which I guess was also kind of daring. Even though I was a lackadaisical student, I graduated when I was sixteen.

In my generation, most everyone in Nicholasville got married after high school. But I had some vague idea of becoming a missionary. Southern Baptists do a lot of missionary work, and I'd heard all about it growing up in the church. I started at the University of Kentucky, but was doing very badly. I think I was just too young and in with a group that believed in cutting classes.

Then one night my high school boyfriend called me from Texas. He was in the Air Force and stationed in San Antonio. He said he was coming home for Christmas and that we should get married. We'd been dating since I was fifteen. I hadn't told my family that I was about to flunk out and thought this was my way to get around that. We didn't believe in being quitters in my family, but I could quit if I were getting married. Of course, I loved him, too.

So I got married when I was eighteen and moved to Texas. My husband was the youngest of five children, and I was the youngest of six. We were both spoiled brats. The marriage only lasted two and a half years. After the divorce, I came back here to Nicholasville.

Then, when I was twenty-two, I moved to Washington, D. C. We had a friend there, and in the fifties it was the acceptable thing for young girls to go to Washington and work for the government. I got a job with a magazine called *The Military Engineer* doing clerical work in the circulation department. I also volunteered for the USO [United Service Organization]. My family always did a lot of volunteering.

During those years, I was a part-time beatnik. I wore black and played chess and bongos. I didn't do drugs. It was all so innocent.

I'd get home from work at five-thirty and go to sleep until ten. Then I'd get up and go to the coffee houses and stay there until four or five in the morning. Afterward, I'd go back home and sleep another hour and go to work again. During the day I did my job and didn't talk about my night scene. The people I worked with would have thought I was wicked!

Then Kennedy was elected President. On Inauguration Day the parade came down Pennsylvania Avenue, and I got to see him. You have to think what a welcome change he was from Eisenhower. We'd had eight years of conservative Republicans and then Kennedy came in, forty-two, handsome and glamorous. The things he talked about were so exciting. People wanted to be involved.

One night lying in bed the idea just came to me to join the Peace Corps. Their office was at Lafayette Park, four or five blocks from where I worked, and I went on my lunch hour. I was so excited. I thought I'd be leaving the next week. All the news stories said they wanted volunteers and were recruiting.

But when I walked into the Peace Corps office and told them I wanted to sign up, the first thing they asked me was if I had a college degree. I said no. Well, sorry. It was that quick, that cold. I was just dashed.

I'd never really wanted anything badly before that I didn't get. My sisters will tell you that I would start campaigning a couple of months before Christmas for a present. I'd say, "I'm going to get a bicycle." None of my sisters ever got a bicycle for Christmas, but I would tell everyone that I was going to get one. And sure enough, I would. Or I'd campaign for a watch. Same thing.

That was part of it. Another part of it was that I had this dull job in D.C., and I thought it would be great to write home and tell everyone, "Well, I'm leaving for the Dominican Republic tomorrow."

After being rejected, I went to George Washington University for a time. But this thing of taking a class here and taking a class there and getting a degree in ten or fifteen years—that wasn't what I wanted to do. I wasn't interested. I was working and couldn't afford to quit. So I just kind of forgot about the Peace Corps. It was a closed door.

In 1966 my dad died, and I moved back home. My sisters and I thought someone needed to live with my mom. It was silly because she was perfectly capable of living by herself, but I came home anyway and stayed with her. During that time we got to be really good friends.

After I moved back home, I worked first at Long John Silver's headquarters in Lexington and then at one of their subsidiary companies, Jerry's Restaurants. I also got engaged to a man named Tom Smith. Even though the engagement didn't work out, we've stayed good friends.

At forty, I fell in love with Syl Yunker. He had three kids from a previous marriage. I'd never wanted kids before, but he was such a great father, he made me think that maybe I could be a mother. My angel Joe came along when I was forty-three.

In my twenties and thirties, I would have been one of those moms who leaves the kid home alone while she goes out and parties. But by the time we got Joe, he was my focus. He's a good kid; I'm really lucky to have him. Even though Syl and I were divorced after four and a half years, Joe and his dad are still really good friends. We're all good friends.

Then in 1983, someone told me about a job opening at the Sargent & Greenleaf lock company—S&G for short—and said I'd be perfect for it. I interviewed with Patsy Gray, who's now one of my best friends. She said she knew right away that I would rise up the ranks, but I'd never been in the position of being on a career path. I'd always been into fun and marriage and stuff like that. I was just glad to have a job in Nicholasville that paid pretty well.

I also had an interview with the chairman. The first thing he told me was that he had no use for anyone under thirty. I thought, wow! Then he asked me if there was something about my life that bothered me, and I said, "Well, I've always been bothered by the fact that I don't have a college degree."

He said, "You know, S&G will reimburse you a hundred percent for an A or a B and eighty percent for a C."

Right when he interviewed me, he told me this. I had that information but thought, well, I can't do it. First of all, I had Joe. He was six when I started at S&G. I'd also just bought this house, which scared me to death—the payments and all. And finally, I was in the process of getting a divorce. So, I just filed that information away.

I started out in administrative services. I'd only been there three or four months when Patsy promoted me to project manager. After a year she made me assistant manager. Then a few years later, I became assistant to the president.

Not too long after this last promotion, the president asked me to attend a seminar in Washington, D. C. I took Joe with me, and my sister Sarah came along to supervise him. This was in March. I remember the assistant to the president of Catholic University was there as well as the assistant for a shipbuilding company. There were about thirty people in all. The instructor asked how many of us had college degrees. About half the people raised their hands. He said, "Well, I'm going to tell the rest of you to get a degree when you go back home. I don't care what you get it in— basket weaving, whatever—but the fact that you have a BA or a BS will help you make more money." So on the way home I told Sarah and Joe that I was going to enroll in school that fall.

I was fifty-four when I started at Spalding University, which is in Louisville and about ninety miles from here. It had a program where you could get a degree by going every third weekend. My sister Bettye Lee agreed to keep Joe when I was gone. He was eleven and, of course, I couldn't leave him alone. Classes were four hours each, and you had one Friday night, two on Saturday and two on Sunday. All the students in my program were older. We stayed in the dorm with the eighteen-years-olds, but we had our own rooms. After thirty-eight years of not being in school, I was scared to death.

My advisor was wonderful. She said that if I wanted to graduate in four years, I shouldn't take any electives. "Be focused," she said. "Get a list of the requirements and do those." Spalding is a Catholic school, and the first two courses my advisor told me to take were world religion and philosophy. When I got my grades, I was thinking I was going to fail both. But when I opened the envelope, I had an A in philosophy and an A+ in religion. Oh my gosh, I started crying.

Then the summer after my sophomore year I began to get discouraged. I even considered quitting. That's when I started thinking about the Peace Corps again. The first thing I did was to phone Information to see if the Peace Corps still existed. I really had no idea whether it did or not. When I found out it did, I called right away and asked them if they took older people. They said there was no age limit. So welcoming this time. So friendly. I told them that I wanted to join when I was sixty-five, after Joe was on his own. They advised me that if I had six years to go, I should get a master's because it would help me when I applied. Peace Corps gave me a reason to finish school.

So many people helped me get my degree. Patsy and my sister Bettye Lee proofread all my papers. And Dee Dee, the receptionist at S&G, helped me with all my drawings for my marketing courses.

It also helped that Joe went to a military school for his high school years. The first year he was gone, I slept down here on the couch every night because I was scared to sleep upstairs alone.

Isn't that silly?

I graduated after four years with a BA in marketing. S&G paid for the entire thing. I specifically chose marketing because it was something they would pay for. By then I was fifty-eight years old.

After I finished my degree at Spalding, I was bored. I started volunteering with Operation Read and working with the R.S.V.P. program—Retired Seniors Volunteer Program. I waited a whole year before I started working on my master's degree. I thought I would hate night school, and I did!

I didn't want just some MBA. What I wanted was a degree in international commerce from the University of Kentucky Patterson School. Again, I chose a major that S&G would pay for. I was really thinking about the Peace Corps, thinking that a degree from there would help me get in. I'd heard about the Patterson School all of my life. It's famous in diplomatic circles, the only school like it within five hundred miles of here.

When I first went to ask about the school, they told me that I should take some undergraduate prerequisites there and see how I did before I applied, even though I'd already finished my B.A. I took one course in the fall and another in the spring. I got an A and a B. That was the first year.

Then I applied. To my surprise, they turned me down. When I asked why, they said they could only take thirty people, or something like that. The truth, I think, is that they thought I was too old. I also hadn't gone to Harvard or Yale; I was local.

Fortunately, I had a mole at the school who told me to write a letter asking if there was an age limit. In my letter to the head of the graduate school, I said that I'd taken these two classes and had done well, and I just wondered if the school had an age limit. I think it was this line that got me in. They were probably afraid I would sue or something. I also had my S&G customers from all over the world write letters recommending me. My friend, my mole at the school, said that they had gotten letters from every-where—Russia, Japan, Africa.

I have to say that once the Patterson School accepted me, they accepted me completely. The staff and the administration—it was like none of that ever happened. Even though I was the oldest student, I felt comfortable there. But unlike Spalding, the classes were at night. Like I said, that was the bad part. At first I took just one course a semester. Then I thought I would take two, but two just about did me in. I didn't feel like doing three hours of classes after eight hours of work. And the courses were hard. I had never had a political science class before. It wasn't fun like marketing was.

Still, everything was hunky dory until it came time for me to graduate five years later. At the Patterson School, you don't write a thesis. You just have an oral examination and a written one. When it came time for the oral, I went into this room with a long table. A professor of my choosing, along with my advisor and the director of the Patterson School, were all sitting at one end. I didn't do well. My professor told me later that she'd never seen anybody so nervous. It was a very intimidating setup. When it was over after an hour or two, they said thanks. A while later, I got this letter saying I hadn't passed. What this meant was that after five years of work, I couldn't get my degree! They told me I could take the oral again in April if I would spend the next several months reading thousands of pages and doing more papers, but I thought to myself, "I just can't. I cannot read all those thousands of pages. That's all there is to it."

All this happened right before Thanksgiving. At my family's annual Thanksgiving get-together, I told my nephew Jack, who is a doctor, about how I hadn't passed. He said that when he was in his residency in Atlanta, besides working at the hospital, he also had two part-time jobs to support his family. He had three kids by then. But when he took his practice examination to be board certified, he, too, had failed. This doctor who had examined him told him he might as well give up, that he was never going to pass the real exam. Although doctors can practice without being board certified, this was really important to Jack. So he called his father that night and asked if he would lend him the money to support his family for a year. He quit the two jobs and spent all his time studying. A year later, he passed.

Jack said that I could do what he had done. But I told him I couldn't read those thousands of pages; I couldn't read a hundred pages a week.

He said, "Can you read fifteen in one day?"

I said, "Sure."

"Okay," he said. "Do that."

If it hadn't been for my nephew Jack and that conversation, I would have called the Patterson School and said forget it.

Instead, I called the Patterson School and told them I would do it. I wrote papers on this, that and the other. And, in April I went to take the examination again. This time there was a small room and a circular table. We were all sitting comfortably, them and me. The conversation was very friendly, a completely different setup. After about thirty minutes, they said, "You passed!" I got my master's in May of 1998.

After getting my degree, I applied to the Peace Corps. When I called to tell them I was ready to start, first question: Education? I said I had just graduated with a master's in international commerce, and we went on from there.

The application itself covers everything in your life; and when you're sixty-five, there's a lot! I had to write a couple of essays. The medical application alone was about ten pages. In the medical part I had to say everything I'd ever had done. I'd had an appendectomy in '59, the doctor long dead. Almost all my doctors were dead. In addition to filling out the application, I had to have a bunion operated on because if you have painful bunions, you can't go.

Then there was the teeth thing. The Peace Corps told me that three of my teeth, which had been capped, had to be either replaced or removed. We went round and round with that. They said I had to have all this expensive dental work done at my expense. I just didn't want to do it. They told me they would take me if I had them pulled, but no dentist would pull them because they have this thing about pulling healthy teeth.

Finally I got an appointment with an oral surgeon. Before going there, I had lunch with Patsy and asked her what I should say. Should I tell the doctor that this is my last hope, that I have been waiting thirty-nine years? And she said, "No, Wini. Just cry."

So I went to the appointment and started telling the surgeon all this stuff about how I'd been waiting thirty-nine years and blah, blah, blah. He said, "No, no, no." Then, I started to cry. He finally agreed: "Okay, okay, I'll do it." That was the last thing.

After I got my application in and my teeth pulled, I had two telephone interviews a month apart. They took about an hour each. The first was pretty general; the second, more specific. They asked, "If you were assigned to an Arab country, would you be comfortable wearing skirts down to your ankles?" Stuff like that. Another question was, "If you went to a place with no Baptist churches, what would you do?" And I said, "Well, Baptists believe that if that happens, you're supposed to start one."

The interviewer said, "Well, if you do, you'll be sent home." That's when I learned that the first purpose of the Peace Corps is to share our culture with another country. The second is to bring their culture back here and promote interaction between us. But no religion. No military. This is so that Peace Corps volunteers will be absolutely, in no way, part of any group trying to reform the country. It's such a great concept.

Next I was given a choice of continents. They said I could go teach in either Africa or the Far East, or I could be a business volunteer in Eastern Europe. I said, "Well, I don't want to teach, so I'll go to Eastern Europe. When I got my acceptance in October '99 telling me I was going to Ukraine, I thought, good grief, where is that? I thought it was Siberia!

After getting the letter, I told S&G that I was going to retire. Of course, they weren't surprised. They'd supported me every step of the way.

Then I shaved my head. Did you ever see that movie *G.I. Jane?* Demi Moore just went *bzzzzzz* with the razor and shaved her head. It was a big step 'cause I always liked my hair dark, but I didn't want to be bothered with coloring it in Ukraine and didn't want that polecat look as it was growing out. My friend Velma Miller, who was having chemotherapy, had been told she was going to lose all her hair. So I said to her, "Let's go and shave our heads! We'll do it together." She was convinced she wouldn't lose her hair and wouldn't do it with me, but, of course, she really appreciated my offer.

My departure date was supposed to be January 1, 2000, but they changed it until January 31st because of Y2K. They didn't want anyone traveling on New Year's Day that year. It was good for me because, by working a little bit into January, I got a whole other year's vacation.

I arrived in Ukraine on February 2, 2000. I didn't even know the Cyrillic alphabet before I left, but I knew that the three months' training I'd have when I got there would help me. We flew from Chicago to Kiev and then took a bus to the city of Cherkassy.

I lived there three months with a Ukrainian family. Have you seen the movie *The Sum of All Fears* with Ben Affleck? A lot of it takes place in Russia, and at one point they say they're going to Cherkassy. It was really filmed in Montreal, though. You wouldn't know that if you didn't watch the credits.

In the beginning, there were thirty-three of us in my group. We ended up with thirty-one. We did everything together, except the language classes, and had training from eight-thirty in the morning until five-thirty at night. We all got really close. In the Peace Corps, your group is really important. Even though after three months you separate, those three months really get you together.

For the rest of my time in Ukraine I was assigned to Kirovograd, which is a pretty river town. I had my own apartment on Lenin Street. My building had five floors. I was on the fourth. There was no elevator, but I was really lucky to have three rooms and a balcony. I had a bathroom with the toilet in one room and the tub in another. I had a real commode. My building was built in 1978 and was pretty modern.

It was really, really cold in the winter and really, really hot in the summer. The snow and ice are sometimes devastating, but the Ukrainian spring is really something special. In the winter they don't shovel the sidewalks, and when thousands of people walk on those two feet of snow and it's freezing out, it turns into all this jagged ice. Very treacherous. The first few weeks there I was falling all the time. I'd brought the wrong kinds of boots. I took boots for snow; I didn't know I should have had crampons for ice.

I lined all my windows with duct tape to keep out the cold. That was one thing the Peace Corps said to take with us. I used it for everything. I even repaired furniture with it. Also, Peace Corps supplied us with those small electric furnaces, so we were lucky.

Last November and December, the city couldn't afford to pay for gas. No heat. Normally, November and December aren't that bad there; January and February are the bad months. But last year it got cold in December, below zero. Children would sit in school with their coats and sweaters on.

As hard as this might seem to imagine, difficulties such as sometimes having no water, no electricity, no heat came to seem trivial and manageable. Just a small part of life, not the huge dilemma that it would have seemed to me in the States. We just coped and moved on.

When the Peace Corps accepted me, my idea was that I would work with small businesses and maybe write business plans. Stuff like that. I am not a teacher—never trained for it, never aspired to be one. So when they told me in February of 2000, "Wini, you're going to be a teacher," I felt like Goldie Hawn in *Private Benjamin* when she said, "I joined a different army."

But with a wonderful Ukrainian teacher named Zoya Rodionova as my mentor, always ready to help with suggestions and ideas, I managed to struggle through. Along the way, I developed a great respect for teachers, who, I am now convinced, have the toughest profession in the world.

I had five sections of economics at a secondary school and met each group of students once a week. The school also asked me to teach conversational English. Even though that wasn't part of my contract—and I later learned that a lot of business volunteers refuse—I accepted.

In the Peace Corps you're assigned one job, but you have enormous latitude in what your secondary projects are. And God, chance, luck, good fortune—whatever you call it—presented amazing ones for me to enjoy.

I decided to have an English club for women so they could practice conversation, just to give them courage. The way the club started was that I noticed that Ukraine is very macho. If there were men in a group, the women wouldn't open their mouths.

I also had a secondary project at Detsky Dome, an orphanage where several other Peace Corps volunteers worked. Detsky Dome means "children's house." There were about a hundred and fifty kids there.

Last October Zoya introduced me to Beth Christensen, this

angel who teaches high school in Minnesota and who was on a two-week visit to Kirovograd. One day I took Beth with me to the orphanage and showed her around. Before leaving to come back to the States, she gave me two hundred dollars for the orphanage to spend however I saw fit. I considered just giving it to the director. But then I thought, what if we had a Christmas party with an American Santa Claus? So I e-mailed Patsy and asked her to look into how much a Santa Claus suit would cost. She talked to my sister Zenie, who said she'd make one. Velma contributed her white fur stole to trim the suit, and Patsy told me she would buy the beard and the wig and ship it to Ukraine as her Christmas present to me.

We got the suit and set a date. I asked the other volunteers for their support because I wanted to get a gift for each kid. First I had to negotiate with the orphanage director, Galina, to allow personal gifts. The orphans don't have personal possessions. Even their clothes are kept in a big communal closet. Galina readily agreed and provided us with the names, sex and ages of each of the children. Then six of us volunteers split up the names to buy the gifts.

Meanwhile, Patsy had started what she called a "beg box" at S&G, and the workers there had contributed another two hundred dollars. My sisters Zenie and Bettye Lee and their missionary circle contributed more. Patsy's sister Bonnie from Fayetteville, West Virginia, also sent money, and one of S&G's customers in Florida sent money. We ended up with about six hundred dollars in all. We did goody bags with a tangerine, a chocolate Santa and candy canes that Bettye Lee got and shipped to me. One of the volunteers, Aaron, played Santa Claus. He learned to say in Ukrainian, "Have you been a good boy? Have you been a good girl?" And Tanya, a friend from my English club who was a broadcaster for Kirovograd radio, also came to the party. She told me later that she was so moved that she cried all the way back to the station.

Right before I left Ukraine last March, I got an e-mail from Beth. She said that she'd been making speeches all winter long about this orphanage in Kirovograd and that she had raised fourteen hundred American dollars. Again, she said I could spend it on the orphans however I saw fit. I thought, "Oh Beth, how can I do this? I'm leaving in a month and a half. I don't have the time."

But Zoya helped me and asked Galina for a priority list of what she needed. Galina said that there were eighty school-age kids at the orphanage and that last winter some of them didn't have shoes. They went to school with heavy socks. She said they needed jeans, too. The orphans were planning a farewell celebration for me, so Zoya and I decided to surprise them at my party with the clothes.

A volunteer went to Odessa, which was about eight hours away, and brought back eighty pairs of shoes. Then we found a dealer who provided us with eighty pairs of jeans. With the money left, we bought hundreds of rolls of toilet paper and cleaning supplies. The money went really far. We also bought school supplies—paper, rulers, scissors, glue. We needed five taxis to get the stuff from my living room to the orphanage!

This wonderful party was on April 12th. I left Ukraine a week later. I was there two years. Besides teaching English and economics and volunteering with the English club and the orphanage, I organized a baseball team and was the travel editor for a Peace Corps newsletter. While I was in Ukraine, Bettye Lee came twice. Joe came twice, and some friends from Florida came once.

I had many conflicting emotions about leaving. On one hand, I wanted and needed to see my Kentucky family. On the other hand, I'd made many friends in Kirovograd and was sad to be leaving them. I never would have imagined that I'd learn to love and feel so at home in a foreign country.

Being in Ukraine was unbelievable, the way the two years passed so quickly. I can't say that Peace Corps was all I dreamed of because this experience was much, much more. I truly had the time of my life! ✍

JOURNAL ENTRY 33

There's a saying from the Talmud:"Every blade of grass has its Angel that bends over it and whispers, 'Grow, grow.'" We all have angels in our lives. Some of us might have more than others, but every person I interviewed had at least one.

When I was arranging my long-anticipated trip to Nicholasville to meet Wini Yunker, my original plan was to fly in and fly right back out again. But Wini insisted on having a dinner party in my honor so that I could meet some of the people who'd helped her on her journey— her wonderful eighty-one-year-old sister Zenie, who makes the best homemade rolls I've ever tasted; Zenie's eighty-eight-year-old husband John, who still knows how to charm a woman; her sister Bettye Lee, who could match wits, I'm certain, with anyone I know; her son Joe, who's as warm and amiable as his mom; her best friend Patsy and Patsy's husband Corky, who both have hearts of gold; along with various other friends and relatives. "I couldn't have done this on my own," Wini said to me again and again. And, of course, she's right.

JOURNAL ENTRY 34

I finally found my voice. It wasn't where I thought it would be. It wasn't what I thought it would be. I thought it would be eloquent and I would find it by letting go. It ended up being more plain than fancy, and I found it by embracing all the messy parts of myself. How could I have ever wanted to write like Gabriel García Márquez or Joni Mitchell? It seems so silly now, all the comparisons. How could I have ever wanted to be someone other than me?

"THE SOUL WOULD RATHER FAIL AT ITS OWN
LIFE THAN SUCCEED AT SOMEONE ELSE'S."

—David Whyte, poet

EPILOGUE

On the last day of April 2003, for the second time since I began writing this book, I woke up. But instead of an angel whispering in my ear (see Introduction), Rainelle Burton metaphorically grabbed me by the shoulders and began to shake me into consciousness. She had no clue she was doing it. She simply told me about her life.

Such is the power of stories.

We are twins, Rainelle and I. On the surface, we seem as unalike as two people can be. Though we're both 5 foot 2, she's 250 pounds; I'm 110. She's dark brown; I'm pinkish gray. She grew up in Black Bottom on the east side of Detroit; I grew up in lily white Westport, Connecticut.

But underneath the surface, we share a common root. Both our stories are tales of disassociation, of distancing ourselves from painful truths. And in both of our lives, this disassociation has had positive and negative repercussions.

On the light side, since we were little girls we've both been able to hold the sphere of our pain in our hands and turn it around 360 degrees. It didn't exactly hurt. It was more of a curiosity than a gaping wound.

On the dark side, because for years we couldn't feel the hurt, we also couldn't navigate our way through it—from insecurity to safety, from confusion to clarity, from absence to presence.

After spending the day with Rainelle, I went back to my hotel room and began writing in my journal. Detailed descriptions of very personal traumas—some of which I've alluded to in this book—came pouring out. Tears were streaming down my cheeks. But whereas in the past I've always dismissed anything bad that happened to me by focusing on what I learned from the experience—or by explaining away other people's behavior—this time I did not. To quote Prospero's words from *The Tempest,* for the first time in my life "this thing of darkness, I acknowledge[d] mine."

Then something miraculous happened. I accepted and embraced the totality of who I am. And the moment I did that, I found my voice.

I didn't conjure up the idea to write about late-blooming women. The idea was a gift, waiting for me in *The New York Times.* I thought I was supposed to use this gift to help others find their calling, find their voices. But the truth is that I wrote this book because I felt like I would die if I didn't. The compulsion to write was that strong.

Before meeting Rainelle, I knew my story connected the dots, made the whole into something greater than the sum of its parts. But I couldn't get the words to spill out. For forty-nine years they were caught in the back of my throat, and I grew so accustomed to them being lodged there that I almost forgot I had something important I wanted to say.

The women I've interviewed have stories worthy of their own books. Their stories stand alone without mine. Even more importantly, their stories made my story possible. But this book, reduced to its essence, is about my journey toward myself. And I hope that in reading it, you have learned whatever it is you need to learn to find your own voice and to see yourself with kind eyes. I hope that you, too, will defy gravity and begin to fly.

APPENDIX A

SOME OTHER NOTABLE LATE-BLOOMING WOMEN

If you still think it's too late for you, here are three dozen more women who discovered their gifts mid-life and beyond. Some are famous; others are not. Each is recognized in her chosen field.

ACTIVISTS

BETTY FRIEDAN was a housewife before publishing *The Feminine Mystique* at age forty-two. At age forty-five, she co-founded the National Organization for Women (NOW).

At age forty-nine, **ELEANOR ROOSEVELT** became one of our most outspoken and politically active First Ladies, fighting for social justice and championing numerous humanitarian causes. In her sixties, she became a delegate to the United Nations and was elected head of the U.N. Human Rights Commission.

At age sixty-five, **MAGGIE KUHN** founded the Gray Panthers to advocate for the rights of retired Americans.

A pediatrician and passionate advocate for peace, **HELEN CALDICOTT** resigned from medicine at age forty-two to devote her energies to the anti-nuclear movement. At age forty-eight, she was nominated for the Nobel Peace Prize.

Born into slavery and illiterate until the age of thirty, **SOJOURNER TRUTH** wrote *The Narrative of Sojourner Truth* at age fifty-three and became a staunch abolitionist and women's rights advocate.

A mother of thirteen children, **JOAN McGOVERN** was a housewife and Realtor when her son Tommy died of AIDS in 1990. The next year, at the age of sixty-five, she and two other women founded The Lord's Pantry, a non-profit organization currently serving more than 2,000 meals a week to homebound AIDS patients, their caregivers and children in the Westchester, New York, area.

ACTRESS

PEG PHILLIPS, who played shopkeeper Ruth-Anne on TVs "Northern Exposure," began acting at age sixty-five after retiring from her job as an accountant.

AMBASSADOR

Socialite **PAMELA HARRIMAN** became ambassador to France at age seventy-three.

ARTISTS

Taking up painting in her late seventies, **GRANDMA MOSES** (Anna Mary Robertson) became one of America's most noted and popular folk artists. Still painting at age ninety-nine, she left behind more than 1,500 works of art when she died at 101.

GERTRUDE BLEIBERG started painting at age fifty after signing up for an adult education class. Some of her highly personal, expressionist works are part of the San Francisco Museum of Modern Art's permanent collection.

ATHLETES

RUTH ANDERSON began her ultra-distance running career at age forty-six. Setting many records, she was voted into the National Masters Track and Field Hall of Fame.

Never considering herself an athlete and among the last to be picked for teams as a child, **MARJORIE BEINFIELD** started throwing the javelin at age seventy-two and won a gold medal at the Connecticut Senior Olympics at age seventy-five.

DIANE COTTING began rowing in her mid-forties. Diagnosed with breast cancer at age forty-eight, she endured nine surgeries and four chemotherapy treatments before going into remission. At age fifty she formed a team of breast-cancer survivors to row in the prestigious Head of the Charles Regatta in Boston.

AUTHORS

PENELOPE FITZGERALD published her first novel at age sixty. Her third novel, *Offshore,* won the Booker Prize, England's most prestigious literary award.

Best-selling author **JUDITH KRANTZ** wrote her first novel, *Scruples,* at age fifty.

Legendary New York philanthropist **BROOKE ASTOR** wrote a well-received first novel, *The Last Blossom on the Plum Tree,* in her late eighties.

After forty-five years as a nurse, **JEANNE RAY** began writing at age sixty. Her captivating first book, *Julie & Romeo,* tells the story of two feisty rival florists, both also in their sixties, who reclaim romance and passion. To date, it has sold more than 480,000 copies! She's gone on to publish two more novels: *Step-Ball Change* and *Eat Cake.*

KATE CHOPIN penned her first novel, *The Awakening,* at age forty-seven.

BROADCASTING REGULATION EXPERT
At age forty-nine, **MARJORIE FERGUSON** was awarded a Ph.D. in sociology from the University of London and taught for a decade at the London School of Economics. For the next ten years, until her death at age sixty-nine, she was affiliated with the University of Maryland and earned a global reputation in the field of broadcasting regulation.

CHEF
Discovering a passion for French cooking while living in France in her late thirties, **JULIA CHILD** wrote her famous cookbook *Mastering the Art of French Cooking* at age forty-nine and became host of the popular PBS series *The French Chef* at age fifty-one.

DESIGNER
Taking over her late-husband's design firm at age sixty, former *House Beautiful* editor-in-chief **SARAH TOMERLIN LEE** became a renowned hotel designer.

DOG TRAINER
Claiming that her life began at seventy, **BARBARA WOODHOUSE** started training dogs after her husband died and found international fame from publishing several books and hosting a popular television program on the subject.

ENTREPRENEUR
At age forty-five, **MARY KAY ASH** started her billion-dollar cosmetics empire from a five-thousand-dollar investment.

ETIQUETTE EXPERT
EMILY POST published *Etiquette,* her best-selling guide to proper social behavior, at age forty-nine.

HORTICULTURALIST
A patron saint of modern gardening, **GERTRUDE JEKYLL** began designing gardens in earnest at age thirty-five and wrote *A Gardener's Testament* at age fifty-three.

NEWSPAPER PUBLISHER
Pulitzer Prize-winning author **KATHERINE GRAHAM** was a full-time wife and mother until age forty-six when her husband, *Washington Post* owner and publisher Philip Graham, committed suicide. Initially shy and insecure, she became

president of the newspaper upon his death and was named publisher at age fifty-two. Under her tenure, the *Washington Post* gained a national reputation for its coverage of Watergate and its publication of the Pentagon Papers.

NUN

A parent of seven and grandmother of twelve, **BEA KELLER,** at age fifty-one, entered the Sisters of Charity of Nazareth, an apostolic order dedicated to social service. She is also the founder of the Sister Moms organization, which currently has 125 members.

OLDER GRADUATES

Earning a high school equivalency diploma at age sixty-five, **ELIZABETH EICHELBAUM** was awarded a doctorate in art therapy from the University of Tennessee at age ninety.

ANNE MARTINDELL graduated from Smith College at age eighty-seven.

PEACE CORPS VOLUNTEER

LILLIAN CARTER, mother of President Jimmy Carter, joined the Peace Corps at age sixty-eight and spent two years in India. The Atlanta regional office of the Peace Corps established an award in her name presented every five years to recognize volunteers fifty and over for outstanding service.

PILOT

BESSIE COLEMAN, the first African-American female pilot, was a manicurist in Chicago until she started flying at age twenty-eight. She performed at countless air shows and developed a national reputation.

POET

SHARON OLDS, whose work has been anthologized in more than a hundred collections and translated into seven languages, published her first volume of poetry at age thirty-eight.

POLITICIANS

TAKAKO DOI entered politics at age forty-one and became Chair of the Japan Social Democratic Party at age fifty-eight.

After her husband Sonny Bono died, **MARY BONO** was elected to Congress at age thirty-seven to fill his seat. In 1999 *George* magazine named her one of the Twenty Most Fascinating Women in Politics.

Gun-control advocate **CAROLYN MCCARTHY,** whose husband was killed and son injured in the Long Island train massacre, was a nurse for thirty years before being elected to Congress at age fifty-two. In 2000 she helped organize the Million Man March.

Former housewife **JULIE BELAGA** became a Connecticut state legislator at age forty-six and the Republican nominee for governor at age fifty-six. She went on to become an administrator for the Environmental Protection Agency and the Chief Operating Officer (COO) of the Export/Import Bank.

RACE CAR DRIVER

LYN ST. JAMES completed her first Indy 500 at age forty-five and was named by *Sports Illustrated* as one of their Top 100 Women Athletes of the Century.

SINGER

Critically-acclaimed jazz singer **ABBEY LINCOLN** was forty years old before composing her first song.

APPENDIX B

SELECTED RESOURCES

If you want to go back to school, change careers or pursue a passion, there are numerous programs and organizations eager to help. I have included the ones specifically referred to by the women in this book below:

THE COLLEGE LEVEL EXAMINATION PROGRAM (CLEP)

The College-Level Examination Program® (CLEP) is a credit-by-examination program that helps students of all ages earn college degrees faster by getting credit for what they already know.

For more information, contact the College Board:
CLEP, P.O. Box 6600, Princeton, NJ 08541-6600 phone: 800-257-9558 e-mail: clep@info.collegeboard.org http://www.collegeboard.com/student/ testing/clep/about.html

EXPERIENTIAL LEARNING CREDITS

Many community colleges and universities award Experiential Learning Credits for college-level learning acquired in a non-traditional setting. Contact the school of your choice for more information.

AMERICAN ASSOCIATION OF COMMUNITY COLLEGES (AACC)

Many community colleges have night and weekend classes. Some, such as the Borough of Manhattan Community College in New York, even hold classes on Saturday evenings. Contact individual schools to find out their schedules.

To locate a nearby community college, contact the AACC:
One Dupont Circle NW, Suite 410, Washington, DC 20036 phone: 202-728-0200 http://www.aacc.nche.edu

BROWN UNIVERSITY RESUMED UNDERGRADUATE EDUCATION PROGRAM (RUSA)

From their website: Resumed Undergraduate Education students at Brown are fully matriculated candidates for the baccalaureate degree. All undergraduate courses are available to them, and once admitted they follow the regular registration procedures of Brown University. RUE students are different from other Brown students only in that they may elect to carry a reduced course load instead of the full load required of other students and in that admission is need-aware, but not need-blind. Therefore, you may find that as a RUE student you can design a course schedule at Brown University compatible with family and job responsibilities you previously considered barriers to a high-quality college education and can, therefore, design a course schedule compatible with family and job responsibilities.

For more information, contact the RUE program: *Office of Undergraduate Admission–Resumed Undergraduate Education, Brown University, Box 1876, Providence, RI 02912 phone: 401-863-2378 http://www.brown.edu/Students/RUSA*

GED (GENERAL EQUIVALENCY DIPLOMA)

The GED testing program provides adults who never completed high school an opportunity to continue their education. About ninety-five percent of colleges accept a GED certificate in lieu of a high school diploma.

From their website: You can take the GED Tests almost anywhere in the United States and Canada, as well as at more than 100 sites internationally. GED Testing Centers can often help to find you instruction so that you're prepared to pass the GED Tests. The GED Tests measure your knowledge and academic skills against those of today's traditional high school graduates.

For more information, contact the Center for Adult Learning Educational Credentials (CALEC): *One Dupont Circle NW, Suite 250, Washington DC, 20036 phone: 939-9475 http://www.acenet.edu/calec/ged/*

ADA COMSTOCK SCHOLARS PROGRAM OF SMITH COLLEGE

Almost 1,800 women have graduated from the Ada Comstock Scholars Program since it was established in 1975 to enable women of non-traditional age to complete a Bachelor of Arts degree. Some adult students at Smith have a complete immersion in the undergraduate, residential student experience; others elect to attend part-time while continuing to juggle family and work responsibilities. The more than 230 current Ada Comstock Scholars comprise a large, valued, dynamic force in the college community.

Ada Comstock Scholars attend the same classes and fulfill the same requirements as traditional-age Smith students. Nearly 90 percent are awarded financial aid and 50 percent live in college housing, including apartments, dorms and commuter rooms. Ada Comstock Scholars range in age from twenty-four to sixty-four (the oldest was eighty-eight when she graduated) and most enter Smith having earned recent credit at community colleges across the country.

For more information, contact Ada Comstock Scholars Program: *Office of Admission, Smith College, Northampton, MA 01063 phone: 800-383-3232 e-mail: admission@smith.edu http://www.smith.edu*

THE PEACE CORPS

Older Americans contribute to Peace Corps programs all over the globe. Currently, 6 percent of Peace Corps volunteers are over fifty; and many older volunteers find their age to be an asset while serving overseas. No single group has more to offer in terms of experience, maturity and demonstrated ability. And because there's no upper age limit to serve, it's never too late. Volunteers who are well into their eighties have served and continue to serve.

Older volunteers work in all areas, including business development; education, youth and community development; agriculture and the environment; and health and HIV/AIDS. The Peace Corps prepares all volunteers with extensive language, technical and cross-cultural awareness training.

For more information, visit their website at http://www.peacecorps.gov or call toll free at 1-800-424-8580, option 1.

OTHER RESOURCES

For links to the above sites, along with other resources for late bloomers, go to http://www.prillboyle.com.

ACKNOWLEDGEMENTS

This book would never have gotten off the ground without the encouragement and support of the following people:

Michael Boyle, my husband and best friend, for believing in me when I didn't believe in myself.

Katarina Jankowski, my "niece," for her honesty, uncompromising ear and invaluable editorial assistance.

Paul Fedorko, my heaven-sent agent, for taking me under his wing.

Richard Hunt, my tireless publisher, for making my dream a reality.

Late bloomers *Susan Baugh, Elizabeth Buzzelli, Susan Hackel, Diane Landau-Flayter* and *Marion Perkus* for opening up their hearts and homes to me. Their stories are every bit as important as the ones I ended up telling.

Carol Cooper Garey, Judith Marks-White, Jane Hammerslough and *Barbara Callahan* for getting me started.

Tamara Meyer, my "partner in boldness," whose vision, intelligence and creativity propelled me onward.

Gabriel Bach, my oldest son, for his wonderful, timely suggestions and artistic spirit.

Everett Boyle, my youngest son, and *Chris Brown*, my dear friend, for being my champions.

Joshua Boyle, my stepson, and *Brianna Carroll*, his fiance, for their shameless enthusiasm.

J. Gilbert Plantinga, my brother, for having the courage to be an artist and leading the way.

Lisa Thurston for her wisdom, healing hands and sharp proofreader's eye.

Pamela Miles for her invaluable guidance and support.

Nancy Drake and *Kathy Krein* for keeping me airborne.

Becky Demarco for her friendship and her art.

Eileen Harrington, Denise Olsen and *Melissa Dobbyn* for serving, however briefly, as my sounding board.

Maryann Palumbo, my straight-shooting publicist, for believing in the book.

Bill Bronrott for his warm heart, intelligence and expert advice.

Elisabeth Weed for her publishing expertise and encouragement.

Mary Jo and *Tom McCann* for offering me their Nantucket refuge when I needed it most.

Martha Sussman, Sheila Papillion and *Betty Hornor* for being my angels.

Julie Belaga and *Philip Bigler* for being my role models.

Homer Allen for coming to my rescue.

Brett Denkin, Steve Gilbert, Jim Hornor, Eileen Hornor, Michael Robinson and *Peter Ulisse* for their friendship and support.

Karen Haughey for her art and inspiration.

Greg Blatman for his generosity of spirit and attention to detail.

Maureen Berger for her editorial assistance.

My team at Emmis: Publicity Director *Howard Cohen,* for his good energy; Design Director *Dana Boll,* for honoring my vision; Editorial Director *Jack Heffron,* for his open mind; and Sales Director *Katie Parker* for her warm spirit.

Suzanne Sheridan, Rozanne Gates and *Penny Pearlman* for helping me cross the finish line.

Authors *Julia Cameron (The Artist's Way)* and *Natalie Goldberg (Writing Down the Bones)* for their inspiration.

Hannelore Hahn for The International Women's Writing Guild (IWWG).

Each of the wonderful women who responded to my ad in the IWWG newsletter.

All the other friends, neighbors, relatives and acquaintances—too numerous to mention—who cheered me on.

And finally, my beloved teacher of thirty years, *Prem Rawat,* for always reminding me to listen to my heart.